CRIMINAL LAW

CRIMINAL LAW
AN INDICTMENT

Richard J. Orloski

nh Nelson-Hall, Chicago

Library of Congress Cataloging in Publication Data
Orloski, Richard J
Criminal law
Includes index.
1. Criminal law—United States. I. Title
KF9219.O7 345'.73 76-28995
ISBN 0-88229-211-0

Copyright © 1977 by Richard J. Orloski

Manufactured in the United States of America.

To the Women in My Life

Contents

Preface

Writing a book is a distillation of many learning experiences. An attempt to thank all those to whom I feel indebted is impossible. Listing particular persons, whose contribution to my own personal learning experience has been invaluable, is always dangerous because a fallible memory is apt to forget several persons whose contributions have been enormous. In any event, I feel compelled to make the effort and apologize now to those who will unintentionally be passed over.

To Professors John Ennis and Clement Valletta of King's College, a warm thanks for their patience and tutelage in my early years in the pursuit of writing. To Professors Robert Alexander and Donald Buzinkai, also of King's, a very special acknowledgment of their instructions in the art of government and the realities of our constitutional system. To Professors Ian Macneil and Ernest Roberts of Cornell Law School, a deep appreciation for having taught me to look behind the mechanics of law and to understand the institutionalized realities that law merely mirrors. Finally, in my academic preparation for this endeavor, to Professor Kurt Hanslowe, also of Cornell Law, who taught me Constitutional and Criminal

Law in a period when both were undergoing dramatic and often traumatic change, my sincere thanks.

In my professional career, I would be remiss if I forgot Bill Beyers, of Cleveland, Ohio. Mr. Beyers was the first criminal trial lawyer to become a friend, and he gave me a perspective on criminal law during my summer with him in the Cleveland Public Defender's Office that only can come with life and experience. There is also N. O. Stockmeyer of Lansing, Michigan, who taught me the subtleties of legal research, an indispensable lesson for any lawyer, especially one who undertakes to write a book. Then there is Bill Anderson of the Pennsylvania Attorney General's Office, whose encouragement and generosity in all things gave me the confidence to feel at ease with the label attorney and counselor at law. Finally, there is George J. Joseph, district attorney of Lehigh County, Pennsylvania, a man of rare gifts and insights, who by his example demonstrated that compassion and firmness can indeed exist side by side in the prosecution of criminal law.

On a more personal note, the deepest indebtedness is owed to my parents who, by extreme effort of will and personal sacrifice, gave me the opportunity to obtain my education. Without that, all other learning experiences would not have happened. Finally, to my wife, Kathy, who spent endless hours alone with the children while I hid in libraries and completed this book, a very special thanks with the promise that I will try to spend more time with her and the kids.

To all, I offer my thanks and gratitude. Any credit must be shared with them, but any shortcomings are purely my own. I caution the reader to bear that in mind while proceeding through these pages, and to express with me a sincere "thank you" to my typist, Kathie Shirilla, who transformed my illegible scrawl into a readable manuscript. If only my words are as good as her typing.

One:

Introduction—
Ignorance Is Bliss

It is difficult to convince a layman that he knows little, if anything, about the realities of criminal law. After all, its details fill the newspapers of every American city every single day. Television and radio news broadcasts fill our airwaves with accounts of crimes, with the progress of trials, and with the verdicts of juries. Fictionalized stories of cops and robbers and exaggerated tales of crafty lawyers are part of our folklore handed down from generation to generation through the medium of movies and television and in the printed word of books and magazines. There is a ubiquitousness about crime in America, and a pervasiveness of the processes of law that allows everyone to feel a sense of familiarity with the assumptions of the criminal adjudicatory system. Innocent until proven guilty. Guilt beyond a reasonable doubt. These are the maxims that every schoolboy can quote by rote, and that every lawyer who ever saw a criminal trial quickly recognizes as myths. Essentially, the public is ignorant about the realities of criminal law, its processes, and its purposes. Until such a time, however, that an informed citizenry understands the rudiments of its procedures and purposes, politicians will continue to campaign for law-and-order, and for reforming our prisons, and nothing will change because ignorance is bliss, and knowledge is the only cure-all.

The television series "Perry Mason" is indicative of the public's unawareness of the realities of criminal law. Anyone who ever watched this television dramatization of Erle Stanley Gardner's fictionalized barrister quickly discerns a repetitious pattern. Mr. Mason represents a person charged with murder. The client is innocent, and, inevitably, Perry Mason frees the accused by disclosing the identity of the real murderer and getting him or her to confess in the courtroom. The television viewer may or may not know that the author, Erle Stanley Gardner, was himself a lawyer. But what only the most learned of laymen will recognize in watching the series, however, is that Mr. Gardner has unconditionally predetermined the result by his selection of the proceeding at which Perry Mason asserts his client's defense. The courtroom drama is almost invariably staged at the preliminary hearing where there is no jury and where the only question before the court is whether or not the prosecution has sufficient evidence to warrant the case being tried by a jury. In other words, if the prosecution has any evidence whatsoever indicating guilt, no matter how disputed by the defense, the judge is obligated by law to turn the matter over to a jury. As a practical matter, therefore, the only real defense is conclusive evidence of the guilt of another party, i.e., a confession by the guilty party. So, Mr. Mason obtains his confession, and, legally, it is the only substantive defense possible in the framework selected by the author.

The observation of Erle Stanley Gardner's faithfulness to legal technicalities is only an incidental within the larger context of the realities of the American system for determining criminal liability. It is significant, however, in indicating the subtleties that escape the casual observer of the criminal-law process, and the importance of the unknown and undetected in determining the results in criminal adjudication.

Former presidential advisor, Daniel P. Moynihan, is reputed to have said that no one knows anything about crime in America. That obviously is overstated. The real problem is to convince the American people just how little they do know, then to teach them the elementaries of a system that is essential in order to establish justice, to insure the domestic tranquillity, to promote the general welfare, and to secure the blessings of liberty to ourselves and our posterity. To begin the lesson, it is necessary to set forth the basic purposes of criminal law.

Criminal law has four primary purposes: (1) retribution, (2) revenge, (3) deterrence, and (4) rehabilitation. Throughout Western man's concept of justice, there runs the common thread of requiring recompense or retribution for acts done by men in violation of their fellow men. The classic formulation was articulated even before the birth of Christ: an eye for an eye, a tooth for a tooth. The Western mind requires a balance, a symmetry, of punishment for injustice in order to yield justice. This premise runs throughout our criminal statutes, though one may very well question what legislators consider the proper balance in the various and sundry offenses. Retribution is, however, only one purpose, and at times, man succumbs to his more base nature and achieves satisfaction only in the more brutal requirements of revenge.

Revenge is not normally considered one of man's more laudatory motivations. In twentieth-century America, it is viewed as crass and vulgar. There was a time when it was not only fashionable and honorable to seek such retaliation, but also a necessary prerequisite to manliness. Such behavior, however, is no longer the norm, and even those who desire revenge attempt to disguise their true yearnings as merely a sophisticated form of retribution. Richard Nixon's position on withholding amnesty for all draft-dodgers, including conscientious objectors, is a classic example of an attempt to camouflage revenge with retributive justice. Nixon colors his absolute disclaim for amnesty with a concern for the millions of brave men who served in Vietnam on behalf of their country, and for the thousands who paid the ultimate sacrifice. Yet, he offers no correlation between amnesty and service to country, and he does not pretend that withholding amnesty will somehow benefit either those who served or those who died. It is, in other words, a thinly disguised quest for revenge in order to obtain a subjective satisfaction for grievances by inflicting unmitigating punishment upon those who violated their country's expectations of them. Any such discussion of amnesty, however, also yields concern about precedents for future wars and yet-unborn young men who might someday be called to serve in them. Such heedfulness is commonly lumped under the generic term of *deterrence*.

Deterrence is one of the most abstract and lofty pursuits in our system of criminal law. Criminal statutes ordinarily do not pretend to prescribe certain forms of human behavior that legislators find reprehensible. A statute making it illegal to kill does not begin by asserting that the intentional murder of human beings "ought not to be" permitted. Instead, such a statute merely recites that a person who intentionally, maliciously, and premeditatedly kills another human being is guilty of first-degree murder. In other words, crime is usually defined in terms of completed behavior, not in the context of prescribing future behavior. Deterrence is supposed to arise because of the general knowledge by the populace that engaging in such activity will produce punishment (if caught), and, therefore, to avoid such punishment, people will be deterred from crime. In short, deterrence is something that everyone assumes criminal statutes ultimately effect without anyone being able to produce empirical evidence that such is the case. Consequently, in any discussion of deterrence achieved through criminal law, one must remember that it is the most abstract and speculative pursuit within our framework of criminal law, and that it is scientifically impossible to establish by empirical data that punishment of a *fait accompli* prevents other people from engaging in future analogous behavior.

After the criminal is caught—and convicted—the fourth purpose, rehabilitation, comes into play. Rehabilitation is probably one of the most noble and idealistic of all assumed purposes of criminal law. Essentially, its premise is that, in time, the human personality, and concomitantly, human behavior, can be changed by the external and internal influences that others have over their fellow human beings. The changes desired, of course, are for the better, as the persons who are attempting to induce change subjectively define "the better."

The attempt at such change only takes place after the offender is caught and convicted of "unlawful" human behavior. "Unlawful" is that which the legislature says it is, and which the courts find a permissible and legitimate interference in human liberty. The legislature can establish that certain activities are unlawful, and the courts can disagree. The classic example of such a disagreement is the dispute over abortion. For years, legislators in their infinite knowledge and wisdom wrote that abortion was contrary to law. For years, the courts agreed. Then, the Supreme Court carved out an exception to the prevailing view and held that only an abortion in the last three months of pregnancy can be considered unlawful. Abortions during the first six months of pregnancy were probably legally permissible, but even that is less than clear in Justice Blackmun's majority opinions in *Roe* v. *Wade* 410 U.S. 113, 93 S.Ct. 705 35L. Ed 2d 147 (1973) and *Doe* v. *Bolton* 410 U.S. 179, 93 S.Ct. 739 35L. Ed 2d 147 (1973).

In any event, rehabilitation is considered an admirable and desirable goal to prevent one of criminal law's biggest problems: recidivism. Essentially, recidivism means that the same people, once released from prison, go out and perform the same or similar illegal acts for which they were put in prison in the first place, and this pattern of repeated criminal behavior by a large, hard-core, criminal populace accounts for a major percentage of crime in America. Although true rehabilitation would appear to be the answer, rehabilitation costs money, and punishment alone does not appear to be sufficient to rehabilitate (or change for the better) our notorious and persistent criminal offenders. The problem may be that placing abnormal people in an abnormal environment and forcing them to live an abnormal life style is not conducive to the desired end of producing normal citizens. More on that later, but for now, it is important to recognize that rehabilitation is considered a legitimate and useful goal in the criminal adjudication system.

Retribution, revenge, deterrence, and rehabilitation are all operating at the same time within the context of our criminal-law process. This does not mean, however, that the four are harmonious. Obviously, if the primary concern is revenge, rehabilitation is not even an incidental consideration. Proponents of capital punishment are not in the slightest bit interested in changing the offender's personality. They simply want him eliminated. Similarly, deterrence can run contrary to retribution. If deterrence is the primary objective, the harshness of punishment becomes more significant than attempting to balance the punishment to fit the crime. The emphasis that the individual places upon one or more of the four purposes is indicative of the philosophy of that person towards crime and criminal law. The hard-nose law-and-order freak is more apt to select exclusively revenge and deterrence whereas the limousine-liberal do-gooder is inclined to talk in terms of rehabilitation and retribution. It must be remembered, however, that all four considerations are legitimate factors to be pursued in our criminal-law system, and the question becomes one of selecting among the four in order that each pursuit receives its legitimate proportionate share of attention. In this manner, an informed citizenry can guide its elected representatives in establishing a criminal-adjudication system that works. Before that can be accomplished, however, the citizenry must understand the basics and subtleties of how the present system functions in order to determine its efficacy and its wisdom, and in order to evaluate the need for reform. With that, one must begin at the beginning, and the criminal-law system commences with the arrest.

Two:

The Arrest—
The Wisdom of
"Probable Cause"

In 1791, the United States Constitution was amended to provide that no person shall be arrested unless a warrant was issued and the warrant based upon "probable cause." The Founding Fathers had experienced firsthand the abuses of uncontrolled executive power. It was their intention to hamstring the executive officer of government because they, like Lord Acton, believed that power corrupts, and absolute power corrupts absolutely. The issuance of a warrant for arrest implied that the executive branch of government be dependent upon convincing a judicial magistrate that the warrant should issue. The standard for the issuance of a warrant was "probable cause." Translated into simplest terms, the officer requesting the warrant must convince the member of the judiciary that the person to be arrested is *probably* guilty of a crime. Technical rules of evidence would come into play after arrest. The sufficiency of the evidence and guilt beyond a reasonable doubt would be subsequent standards to be applied at the trial of the accused. For purposes of the arrest, probable cause was the constitutional standard in 1791, and remains the standard today. Its wisdom was to be exemplified in the Detroit shoot-out of 1972.

It was a warm spring night in Detroit in 1972 when five off-duty sheriff's deputies gathered together at midnight to play a few hands of poker at a west side Detroit apartment. The job of a sheriff's deputy in Detroit mostly involved transferring prisoners between prison and court, and guns were a normal part of the work routine and the deputy sheriff's life style. There was at least one gun in the room of assembled lawmen that early morning, and the door to the apartment was intentionally left ajar to allow the breeze to refreshen the night.

Back in March 1972, the Detroit police department was experimenting with a special elite squad of trouble shooters who bore the ominous appellation, STRESS (Stop The Robbers—Enjoy Safe Streets). Those diligent STRESS officers noticed the deputies' harmless card game and the shoot-out began. Conflicting tales will never allow anyone to recreate with certainty the sequence of events involved in the shoot-out that night of March 10, 1972. Subsequent investigation, however, revealed at least 100 rounds of double-barrel buckshot magnum fired by the Detroit police, three sheriff's deputies wounded, and one sheriff's deputy dead. It was city law officers against county law officials, and only one thing was certain. The constitutional standard of probable cause was abrogated, but if it had been followed, the dead would have remained alive. The police officers had no reason to believe that a crime was in progress. There was no warrant issued for the arrest of the card-playing deputies. STRESS officers were certainly not justified in entering the apartment, unannounced, with shotguns blazing.

Lest one be too harsh in sitting in judgment of those overzealous STRESS officers, however, it is noted that a jury of their peers would subsequently acquit the three policemen of all criminal wrongdoing stemming from that episode. Furthermore, it is good to be reminded of what Gilbert Keith Chesterton once wrote of a different time but of similar people:

> The horrible thing about all legal officials, even the best, about all judges, magistrates, barristers, detectives and policemen, is not that they are wicked (some of them are good), not that they are stupid (some of them are quite intelligent), it is simply that they have got used to it.

No one can ever justify the Detroit shoot-out in 1972. Of course, police officers are not obligated in all instances to obtain a warrant to make an arrest. The classic formula is that police officers can arrest anyone *without a warrant* for a felony where the officer has probable cause to make the arrest, but that same officer can only arrest without a warrant for a misdemeanor where the offense is committed within the view and presence of the arresting officer. This felony-misdemeanor distinction for arrests without warrants has caused many technical problems. Take, for example, the situation where the policeman is called to the scene of an automobile accident. Upon his arrival, he finds one of the drivers of the automobile absolutely drunk. The driver reeks of alcohol. He cannot stand without falling. His speech is slurred. He is loud, boisterous, and, at times, vomiting. The officer interviews the other driver and quickly concludes that the drunken driver caused the accident. If, however, the offense of drunken driving in that particular jurisdiction is a misdemeanor, the test of "arrest for misdemeanor in view" would absolutely prohibit the officer from arresting the drunken driver for driving while under the influence of alcohol because the policeman did not actually see the drunken man driving the car. There is no problem with probable cause.

The officer had more than one reason for believing that the drunken driver had just previously driven an automobile while under the influence of alcohol, but the fact that the policeman did not actually view the offense, that is, see the drunken man driving the automobile, prevents the officer from making the arrest on the scene. Instead, the officer must go to a member of the judiciary, explain the facts that lead him to suspect that the man has probably commited a crime, and then request that a warrant be issued for the arrest of the drunken driver. The officer must then take the warrant back to the scene of the accident, or wherever else he might locate the suspect, serve him with the warrant, and then take him into custody, thereby formally placing him under arrest. In the event that this procedure is not followed, and in the event that the jurisdiction involved adheres to the "arrest for misdemeanor in view" test, the failure to follow the exact sequence described above jeopardizes the arrest and allows a sharp defense lawyer to have the entire case dismissed.

Because the classic formulation of arrest on probable cause *without a warrant* for felonies alone, and arrest on probable cause *without a warrant* only for misdemeanors committed in view of the officer proved cumbersome in practice, many states abolished the distinction and instead provided that the arrest need not be by warrant so long as probable cause is satisfied.

It is worthy of note that the Detroit shoot-out occurred not because the warrant requirement of the Bill of Rights was abrogated but mostly because there simply was no probable cause. In the final analysis, "probable cause" depends on the good judgment of the officer making the on-the-scene arrest and of the minor judiciary members issuing the warrant where the arrest proceeds by warrant. Without this good judgment—without their sound common sense, the entire criminal adjudicatory system falls flat on its face, for the system depends on the sound discretion of the police who walk the streets and on the magistrates who issue the warrants of arrest, and if the police cannot be trusted, the criminal adjudication system simply stops. The courts can check the abuses of discretion of policemen and magistrates who improperly issue warrants by throwing out cases where there was no probable cause to make the arrest. Assume, for a moment, that the police for no reason whatsoever stop an automobile and conduct a search. Thereafter, the officers uncover a trunk-load of illegal drugs and arrest the driver and passengers for the illegal trafficking in drugs. On an appropriate motion, the court would review the circumstances of the arrest, and, under these facts, any judge adhering to the United States Constitution would dismiss the drug charges as premised in an illegal arrest because of want of probable cause for the initial stop of the automobile. This resolution is the only one consistent with the mandate of adhering to the constitutional requirement of arrests only for probable cause. But this solution only checks an unwarranted abuse of the arresting power. It does not in any way contribute affirmatively to the massive chore of going out and arresting people who violate the law. It is a simple fact of life that judges do not go out and arrest people. That function is left for the police, and it can be, as all know, a dangerous way to make a living. Given this reality, the courts often give great leeway to the judgment of police officers in on-the-street situations as is evidenced by the Warren court's opinion in *Terry* v. *Ohio*, 392 U.S. 1, 88 S.Ct. 1868, 20 L.Ed. 2d 889 (1968).

On October 31, 1963, Cleveland Police Detective Martin McFadden was patrolling in civilian clothes in downtown Cleveland near the corner of Huron Road and Euclid Avenue at approximately 2:30 P.M. when he noticed two suspicious-looking males walking back and forth on Huron Road. Officer McFadden could not articulate the reason why he picked these two males out of the crowd, later identified as John W. Terry and Richard Chilton, but in his thirty-nine-years' experience on the Cleveland Police Department, he had developed certain routine habits of observation that instinctively led him to detect crime before it happened. As Officer McFadden subsequently testified before the Ohio trial court, "Now, in this case, when I looked over, they didn't look right to me at the time."

Given this instinctive sense of impending crime, Detective McFadden set up a post of observation in the entrance to a store 300 to 400 feet away from Terry and Chilton. He observed one of the two men walking on Huron Road, past some stores, but pausing for a moment and peering into a particular store window. Then, the man continued walking for a short distance, turning around to rejoin his companion on the nearby corner, but once again pausing briefly to look into the same store window. When he rejoined his comrade, the two conferred briefly, and then the companion went through the same series of motions, including the abbreviated walk down Huron Road, inspecting the same store, walking on for a short distance, once again returning to the corner and glancing sheepishly into the store window again as he returned to confer with the first man. The two men repeated this same ritual alternately between five and six times apiece. While Terry and Chilton were standing together on the corner, an unidentified third male approached them and spoke briefly with them. This man, later identified as Carl Katz, then left the two and proceeded west on Euclid Avenue. Terry and Chilton resumed their reconnoitering for an additional ten to twelve minutes, and then walked off together down Euclid Avenue, apparently off to join Katz.

The sequence of events by Terry, Chilton, and Katz made Detective McFadden thoroughly suspicious. The feigned casual reconnaissance of the store on Huron Road intuitively led the detective to believe that the two were "casing a job" and that a stickup was inevitable. The detective followed them cautiously suspecting that they probably had a gun, and he next observed Terry and Chilton approaching Katz in front of Zucker's store. Deciding to pre-empt the suspected robbery, Detective McFadden approached the three men, identified himself as a police officer, and asked for their identification. At this point, the detective's knowledge was confined to the reconnaissance that he observed, and it was conceded that the facts of his observations were not sufficient to satisfy the requirement of probable cause to arrest for a robbery. When the three men refused to answer his inquiry and merely mumbled something in response, Detective McFadden grabbed Terry, spun him around so that Terry was facing his accomplices with Terry being used as a shield between the policeman and the two other suspects. The detective patted down the outside of Terry's clothing and felt a pistol in the left breast pocket of Terry's overcoat. McFadden attempted to remove the gun, but was unable to get it out of the coat pocket. Still keeping Terry between himself and the others, the detective directed all three to enter Zucker's store where he removed Terry's overcoat in order to extricate the gun from the coat pocket. With Terry's gun in hand, the detective proceeded to pat down Chilton and Katz, and found another gun on Chilton. Of the three, only Katz was unarmed. McFadden then asked the proprietor of the store to call for a police wagon that took all three men to the police station where charges of carrying concealed weapons were lodged against Terry and Chilton. Katz was released because the premature arrest evaporated any robbery charges that presumably may have been brought were it not for Detective McFadden's pre-emptive action. At the trial on the concealed-weapons' charges, the guns were introduced as evidence over the objection of defense counsel that the guns were seized as the result of an unreasonable search and seizure. After conviction at trial, the matter ultimately wound its way up the appellate ladder until it came to rest before the United States Supreme Court.

In his majority opinion disposing of the case, Chief Justice Earl Warren candidly admitted that the "stop-and-frisk" was indeed a seizure of Terry's body and a search of his person. The court further agreed that the facts as recited to the trial court by Detective McFadden were not sufficient to satisfy the constitutional requirement of probable cause to make the arrest. As Chief Justice Warren observed, the probable cause for the arrest was not satisfied until after the detective seized the guns. Under this logic, therefore, the initial stop-and-frisk was unwarranted, and the seizure of evidence at the illegal arrest was not properly admissible in a court of law. This was precisely the result that Justice William Douglas thought appropriate on the facts of the case and he expressed this view strongly in dissent. Justice Douglas, however, was the lone dissenter, and the majority agreed with Chief Justice Warren that the stop-and-frisk was a justifiable police investigative technique where there was suspicious behavior that initially attracted police attention. By so holding, the Warren Court made stop-and-frisk a special category of arrest that was not bound by the constitutional prerequisite of probable cause. The primary justification for this constitutional exception was that the safety of the policemen during on-the-street confrontations was a paramount consideration and that the multiplicity of guns on the street necessitated the abrogation of probable cause in the stop-and-frisk situations.

In reality, there are now two types of arrest: stop-and-frisk for suspicious behavior, and arrest with or without warrant for probable cause. In *Terry* v. *Ohio, supra,* the policeman's suspicions were well founded and the court upheld the arrest and conviction. The actions of the STRESS officers in the Detroit shoot-out of 1972, however, were not justified either under the standard of suspicious behavior or probable cause, and hence, they were summoned to account for their actions before a jury of their peers in a criminal prosecution. Both situations typify the necessity for relying on the sound discretion of the police; the hazards where discretion is abused and the rewards where police intuition pre-empts serious crime. In the final analysis, the police form the bulwark in the fight against crime, and crime prevention is merely as good—or as bad—as the police who walk the streets. Adherence to the constitutional principles relies, in the first instance, on the diligence of the police, and where the police act in accordance with law, the judiciary stands ready to support their efforts. Where officers of the law act in violation of their constitutional and statutory duties, however, the judiciary is the only available check to redress the wrong that lawmen effect in the course of enforcing still other laws. In a democratic society, police cannot be a juggernaut, responsible to no other authority. The same, however, is true for the courts, and justice in the criminal adjudicatory system requires judicial deference to the police. The problem lies in the balance that can only be found on a case-by-case basis. Part of the balance is found in court rulings on police searches and seizures, and an in-depth examination of the reasonableness requirement of the Fourth Amendment is now appropriate.

Three:

Search and Seizure, Not Search and Destroy

It was a chilling Tuesday morning in Winthrop, Massachusetts, on January 9, 1973, as Mrs. William Pine attended to her ill thirteen-year-old daughter. The young girl had stayed home from school that day with a mild cold. Bill Pine was working the night shift and was still asleep nestled warmly in his bed at ten that morning when he was awakened by the screams of his wife and child. The front door of the house came crashing down and fifteen state and federal officers came racing through the gaping doorway. One of the lawmen quickly wound his way upstairs and shoved a gun next to Bill Pine's temple. There was no exchange of identification, and the thirteen-year-old girl, near hysteria, pleaded with the men for her life. It was not until Bill Pine finally thrust his own identification into his watchman's face that the error was discovered. The officers had misread the search warrant and invaded the wrong house. They left quietly, without apology, although one of the fifteen did return later that day to offer his regrets and explain that they intended to search the neighboring house, not the Pine residence. It was a short, tragic mix-up, without any adverse long-term consequences. Others would not be so fortunate.

Don Askew and his wife, Virginia, were enjoying a late Monday dinner in their comfortable suburban home in East St. Louis, Illinois, on April 23, 1973, when Mrs. Askew noticed a stranger staring through one of the windows, with a gun prominently displayed. She called to her husband, when, without warning, a nailed-shut screen door came crashing to the ground followed by some twenty-five armed policemen who came pouring into their home. Mrs. Askew fainted in fright, and was spared the burden of seeing her home damaged and her husband shackled like a common criminal. This time, no one accused the police of misreading the address on the search warrant for there was no warrant to be read. It was, however, a mistake for which the law officials offered no apologies. They simply faded back into the night to search the intended residence, leaving Mrs. Askew to undergo a period of hospitalization caused by the trauma of that night.

On the same Monday evening of April 23, 1973, the fifteen policemen who erroneously raided the Giglotto residence in nearby Collinsville, Illinois, would prove to be less gentle. Herbert and Evelyn Giglotto retired early for a long, restful night's sleep. Mr. Giglotto was a solid citizen who began work in the wee hours of the morning so he customarily retired early. At 9:30, that fateful April night, his sleep was disturbed by the sound of his front door being smashed to the floor. Some fifteen police officers suddenly descended upon him, threw him face down into the bed, and handcuffed his arms behind his back. One of the officers towered menacingly over him with a gun, cursed him and his wife, and threatened to end his life. When Giglotto attempted to explain, the officer cocked his gun and vowed to make good on his threat if further statements were offered. None of the men involved in the raid wore a police uniform. On the contrary, they were dressed in the typical undercover garb of dirty jeans and high boots, and were unshaven. None of the men identified himself as a policeman. Mrs. Giglotto wore only a negligee that night, and one of the policemen had the decency to cover her with a sheet as he cursed her for her adulterous relationship with the alleged criminal. When she explained that she was his wife, Evelyn Giglotto only received further verbal abuse. The other officers thoroughly searched the premises, destroying anything that their hands touched. Bookshelves were ripped from the wall. Clothing was torn out of closets and dresser drawers, and heaped together on the floor. A television set, an antique plaster dragon, and expensive cameras were demolished. Again, the mistake was not attributable to a wrong address on the warrant for there was no warrant. When the mistake was discovered, no apologies or regrets were offered. The policemen just faded into the darkness still threatening the Giglottos to remain silent about the episode.

Such erroneous invasions of citizens' private homes are far less infrequent than one would imagine or hope to be the case. An eight-week investigation by the *New York Times* revealed that Mrs. Laura Smith of Chicago, Illinois, Mrs. Anna Majette of Portsmouth, Virginia, Mr. and Mrs. James Herman of Rochester, New York, Mrs. Lilian Davidson of Norfork, Virginia, Mr. Dick Dickinson of Eureka, California, Mrs. Laurette Whitney of Washington, D.C., and Mr. Heywood Henry Dyer of Whittier, California, all underwent similar indignities at the hands of excessive and erroneous police searches. Mrs. Herman was ordered out of the bathtub when the police unlawfully searched her residence. Dick Dickinson was shot and killed by police as he fled from their view. Heywood Henry Dyer was killed accidentally as he cradled his infant son in his hands. Sometimes, however, the police became their own victims as in the case of a Norfork policeman who was shot and killed by a Mrs. Davidson as he came, unannounced, crashing through her door. In all cases, it was a policeman's error—human error—that caused varying degrees of unnecessary human anguish.

The Fourth Amendment is clear and explicit in its command:

> The right of the people to be secure in their persons, houses, papers, and effects, against *unreasonable* [italics added] searches and seizures, shall not be violated, and no warrants shall issue but upon probable cause, supported by oath or affirmation, and particularly describing the place to be searched, and the person or things to be seized.

In order to satisfy the Fourth Amendment, six prerequisites must be met: (1) a warrant must be issued by a member of the judiciary, (2) the person to be searched must be identified, (3) the place must be specified, (4) the property that is being sought must be identified, (5) the facts the police officer knows that suggest that there is *probably* a violation of law must be spelled out, and (6) the search must be reasonable. Given this exacting constitutional standard the courts have ruled that there are certain limited exceptions to the requirement of judicially issued search warrants, namely, where there is consent to the search or where the search is preceded by a lawful and valid arrest, no search warrant is required if exigent circumstances are present but the constitutional premise of "reasonableness" remains. For it must be remembered that the purpose of search and seizure is to obtain evidence to be used at trial, not to destroy the suspect's place of abode in the process of conducting a search.

Where a suspect voluntarily consents to the search of his person or premises, no search warrant is required since the person is deemed to have waived the requirements of the Fourth Amendment. Where the search is limited to property, the owner's consent is all that is needed to waive the requirement of a search warrant, and if evidence of a crime is found against a nonowner during that search, the search is legally valid even though there was no warrant. This principle is illustrated by the recent Supreme Court opinion in *United States* v. *Matlock* 415 U.S. 164, 94 S.Ct. 988, 39 L.Ed. 2d 242 (1974). William E. Matlock was living with Gayle Groff, her three-year-old daughter, and her parents in a house leased by Gayle Groff's parents. When the police arrived, they by-passed Matlock and instead asked Gayle Groff if they could search the premises. Gayle Groff, allegedly the common-law wife of Matlock, consented to the search, including the upstairs bedroom where Matlock slept. In the bedroom closet, the police uncovered $4,995 in cash that was traced to a recent bank robbery. The officers then returned to the front yard and arrested Matlock for the robbery. Prior to trial, Matlock petitioned the trial court to suppress the evidence as the fruit of an illegal search since no warrant was used in searching Matlock's bedroom. The trial court refused the request, and Matlock was thereafter convicted at trial with the $4,995 being used as the major portion of the evidence against him. On appeal to the United States Supreme Court, Matlock reiterated his argument that his conviction was improper because it was based on evidence seized without a search warrant. The Supreme Court disagreed pointing out that Gayle Groff, as the common-law wife of Matlock, was a co-owner of the bedroom in which they slept, and she could properly consent to the search of her bedroom. Failure to obtain Matlock's consent to the search, or failure to obtain a warrant, therefore, became irrelevant since the consent of one of the owners of the property was all that was required to vindicate the search.

The issue of the voluntariness of the consent is always raised in such cases. If the consent is involuntary, then it is ineffective to justify the search. Voluntariness, however, is a question of fact that the trial courts must preliminarily determine before ruling on the validity of a consensual search. In *Schneckloth* v. *Bustamonte*, 412 U.S. 218, 93 S.Ct. 2041, 36 L.Ed. 2d 854 (1973), defense lawyers argued that consent cannot be considered voluntary unless the police also affirmatively advise the person giving the consent that refusal to allow the search is always an option and that the police can be forced to obtain a warrant. The United States Supreme Court rejected this mechanical test for determining the voluntariness of such consent, and instead held that the voluntary character of the consent must be determined from the "totality of the circumstances." As a practical matter, the "totality of the circumstances" test means putting the police officers on the stand to explain how the consent was obtained and allowing the trial court to base a ruling thereon, even where the person who allegedly gave such consent denies ever doing so. Indeed, this is precisely what transpired in *United States* v. *Matlock, supra*. The police testified at a pretrial hearing on the matter that Gayle Groff consented to the search, but Gayle Groff denied under oath that she ever gave such authorization to a search of her bedroom. The trial court believed the testimony of the police and disbelieved Gayle Groff. By making this factual determination, the court was able to justify the search as reasonable based upon the voluntary authorization given by Gayle Groff.

The next major judicial exception to the warrant requirement is the search incident to a lawful arrest. This principle is illustrated by two similar cases treated dissimilarly prior to a ruling by the United States Supreme Court: *United States* v. *Robinson*, 414 U.S. 218, 94 S.Ct. 467, 38 L.Ed. 2d 427 (1973) and *Gustafson* v. *Florida*, 414 U.S. 218, 94 S.Ct. 488, 38 L.Ed. 2d 456 (1973).

Willie Robinson, Jr., was driving his 1965 Cadillac near the intersection of 8th and C Streets, S.E., in Washington, D.C., on April 23, 1968, when he was stopped by a policeman who had probable cause to believe that Robinson was driving his automobile after his driver-license privilege had been suspended. Driving while under suspension is a crime in Washington, D.C., for which the officer could lawfully arrest Robinson. The officer signaled the driver to pull over, and Robinson obliged and stepped out of his vehicle. The policeman immediately placed Robinson under arrest on the motor-vehicle violation and patted him down in what was described as a routine body search. Up to this point, no warrant had been issued for Robinson's arrest and no search warrant had been obtained. During the course of the frisk, the officer uncovered a cigarette packet containing fourteen gelatin capsules bearing white powder that the policeman correctly believed to be heroin. Robinson was convicted by the trial court of possession of heroin based upon the officer's discovery of the capsules in the search. On appeal to the United States Court of Appeals, the conviction was reversed because the court held that a *warrantless* search of a person on a motor-vehicle violation is limited to an investigative stop-and-frisk for weapons in order that the officer might protect himself. No weapons having been uncovered, the policeman could not continue the full body search to find evidence of still another, unrelated crime. Within that framework, the matter was appealed to the United States Supreme Court.

At about the same time the United States Court of Appeals was deciding Willie Robinson's case, the Supreme Court of Florida was hearing the appeal of James E. Gustafson convicted for possession of marijuana cigarettes. On January 12, 1969, at approximately 2 A.M., Gustafson was driving his 1953 white Cadillac in Eau Gallie,

Florida, when a policeman noticed the automobile weaving back and forth across the center yellow line. The officer pulled the vehicle over, and the driver obligingly came to a halt. When asked for his driver's license, Gustafson was unable to produce one because he had left his operator's license in his college dormitory room in nearby Melbourne. The officer then placed Gustafson under arrest for driving without an operator's license in his possession, a motor-vehicle offense under Florida law. Again, at this time, the policeman had no arrest or search warrants for Jim Gustafson. The officer then proceeded to pat down Gustafson for weapons, as well as the passenger in his automobile although all conceded that the passenger was not under arrest and being charged with no crime. During the frisk, the officer discovered no weapons, but instead found a Benson and Hedges cigarette box that the policeman quickly realized contained marijuana cigarettes. No marijuana was found on the passenger. Jim Gustafson was tried and convicted in Florida for the illegal possession of marijuana that had been seized from his person during the arrest for the motor-vehicle violation. Defense counsel made the familiar argument that a *warrantless* search of the body in an investigative stop-and-frisk situation is limited to a search for weapons. Not having found any, the police could not lawfully search the person without a judicially sanctioned warrant to uncover evidence of still another, unrelated crime—to wit, the possession of marijuana. The Florida Supreme Court rejected this argument and sustained Gustafson's conviction. Within this context, the case was appealed to the United States Supreme Court.

When *United States* v. *Robinson, supra,* and *Gustafson* v. *Florida, supra,* reached the United States Supreme Court, the Burger court, speaking through Justice Rehnquist, had little difficulty in validating police action in both cases. Relying upon the traditional exception of the warrant requirement of the Fourth Amendment that searches incident to arrest need no prior judicial sanction, the Supreme Court held that, once arrested, the search without warrant was proper even though there was no danger to the police by discovery of weapons or other exigent circumstances that required a total body search. The thrust of both opinions is that it is reasonable under any and all circumstances to make a full body search of the arrestee, no matter how minor the offense for which the person is originally arrested, and the constitutional stricture of judicially ordered search warrants no longer applies after arrest. This logic would be carried through in other Burger court opinions on the question of the reasonableness of warrantless searches and seizures.

In *Cardwell* v. *Lewis*, 417 U.S. 583, 94 S.Ct. 2464, 41 L.Ed. 2d 325 (1974), the concept of a warrantless search incident to an arrest despite exigent circumstances was extended from the person's body to the exterior of an arrestee's automobile. On July 19, 1967, the body of Paul Radcliffe was found near his automobile on the banks of a river in Delaware County, Ohio. The car had crossed the embankment resting near the brush where Radcliffe was then shot with a shotgun. Plaster casts were made of all tire tracks in the area, and paint samples were scraped from the rear fender of the decedent's automobile. Police immediately suspected that a vehicle was used to shove Radcliffe's automobile off the road where the victim was then shot as he attempted to flee from his automobile. Arthur Lewis became an immediate suspect because of his relationship with the deceased. Radcliffe was an accountant by profession, and he had been hired to review for financial soundness the books of a company that Lewis was trying to sell. On the same day of death, at about 9:30 A.M., a man claiming to be Radcliffe placed a call to the would-be purchaser to advise him that the books were in order. Investigation revealed, however, that the accountant was killed between 8:00 A.M. and 8:30 A.M. that day. Paul Radcliffe was already dead, therefore, at the time he was allegedly giving financial information, which was beneficial to Arthur Lewis, and detrimental to the purchaser. Lewis had apparently killed the accountant in order that the sale of his company might go through unimpeded.

On October 10, 1967, at eight in the morning, the police obtained a warrant for Arthur Lewis's arrest charging him with first-degree murder. When Lewis appeared at the police station two hours later in response to a police request that he voluntarily appear, the officer concealed the fact that a warrant was already issued for his arrest and instead questioned him for seven hours prior to serving the arrest warrant. Upon making the arrest, Lewis's car keys and parking-lot stub were released to the police and a tow truck was dispatched to remove his automobile to the police impoundment lot. No warrant was served to search the vehicle.

Although no search warrant was issued, the police technician thoroughly examined the exterior of Lewis's automobile matching tire tracks with those found at the scene and comparing the paint samples from Lewis's car to the smudge marks found on the deceased's automobile. Such circumstantial evidence, seized without a search warrant, was admitted into evidence at Lewis's trial at which Arthur Lewis was convicted of first-degree murder. On appeal to the United States Supreme Court, the Court in an opinion by Justice Blackmun validated the warrantless search despite the dissent's objection that a warrant could easily have been obtained. Again, the rationale was that, after arrest, a search of an exterior of an automobile is reasonable as incident to a lawful arrest.

This same exception to warrantless searches of automobiles where the defendant is placed under arrest was used in *Cady* v. *Dombrowski*, 413 U.S. 433, 93 S.Ct. 2523, 37 L.Ed. 2d 706 (1973) to justify the search of the interior of an arrestee's car. On September 11, 1969, Chester Dombrowski, a Chicago police officer, was driving his automobile near Kewaskum, Wisconsin, when his 1967 Thunderbird broke through a guardrail and smashed into a bridge abutment. An investigation by the local Wisconsin officer indicated that Dombrowski was driving the vehicle under the influence of alcohol. At the scene, Dombrowski advised the police that he was a Chicago policeman, apparently in an effort to appeal to the arresting officer's fraternal instincts. The gambit failed, and instead caused the officer to search for the service revolver, which the Wisconsin policeman erroneously believed all Chicago lawmen must carry at all times. A search of Dombrowski's person and the front seat and glove compartment of his automobile uncovered no revolver. The Thunderbird was thereafter hauled off to a privately owned garage, and Dombrowski was taken into police custody for drunken driving. Some two hours later, without securing a search warrant, the Wisconsin policeman returned to the Thunderbird, now parked in the private garage, to renew his efforts at finding the supposedly missing service revolver. The officer opened the door of the car and found a blood-stained flashlight. He then examined the trunk, still without a warrant, and discovered more blood-covered items, including a police nightstick and car mat with the blood still fresh. Subsequent investigation produced the body of Herbert McKinny on a far corner of a farm owned by Dombrowski's brother. The bloodstained items, seized without a warrant, were used in a chain of circumstantial evidence leading to Dombrowski's conviction of first-degree murder. Dombrowski challenged the seizure of the evidence without a warrant and the matter finally rested before the United States Supreme Court for disposition. Again, the Supreme Court, in an opinion by Justice Rehnquist, held that the search was justified even though there was ample time to obtain a warrant and even though there were no emergency circumstances requiring the policeman to return to a privately owned garage to search an unattended automobile late at night. Again, the rationale of the Supreme Court was that, once arrested, a person and the exterior and interior of his automobile can be searched without a warrant despite the clear language of the Fourth Amendment to the contrary.

Given the Burger court premise that warrantless searches of persons and their automobiles are permissible when incident to a lawful arrest even though a search warrant could have been obtained, it was only logical that this principle would ultimately be extended to other personal effects. On May 31, 1970, at approximately 11 P.M., Eugene Edwards and Bill Livesay were arrested by federal agents in Lebanon, Ohio, for attempting to break into the local post office. The investigation revealed that the two attempted to gain entrance into the building by prying open a painted wood-framed window, which caused wood chips and splinters to be scattered about the scene of the crime. The next morning, the arresting officers purchased substitute clothing for Edwards and seized the shirt off his back and the trousers from his person as evidence against him. A chemical examination of the clothing uncovered painted wood chips similar in character to the painted wood-framed window at the Lebanon post office building. The clothing and wood chips seized therefrom were offered in evidence against Edwards over his objections that the warrantless search and seizure hours after the arrest and not spatially related thereto was invalid because a search warrant could have been obtained. Again, the Supreme Court rejected the argument and held that a person's personal effects could be searched after arrest as incident thereto even though no warrant had been obtained and even though the search took place hours after the arrest and was not spatially related to the arrestee's person. With this decision in *United States* v. *Edwards*, 415 U.S. 800, 94 S.Ct. 1234, 39 L.Ed. 2d 771 (1974), the cycle was complete. Despite the fact that the Fourth Amendment requires a warrant to search a person, his property, or his effects, the United States Supreme Court has ruled that a search incident to a lawful arrest waives the necessity of a judicially issued search warrant.

The traditional exception of searches incident to a lawful arrest from the constitutional mandate of obtaining search warrants has always been that—an exception. Historically, the exception was judicially applied only when "exigent circumstances" militated against obtaining a warrant. An on-the-scene search of a person and his immediately surrounding environs was permissible as incidental to the arrest. The police officer ought to be allowed to protect himself and search, without a warrant, for a gun that the arrestee might have on his person or have ready access thereto. Also, the policeman ought not to be prevented from seizing evidence of a crime that the arrestee or his accomplices might otherwise destroy if not seized immediately by the police. Such were the tests historically required to obtain the benefit of the search incident to a lawful arrest without a warrant. Under the Burger court view, the language of the Fourth Amendment requiring search warrants is superfluous and the exception permitted to gobble up the rule. Once arrested, the person and his property and effects can be searched without a warrant. Willie Robinson, Jr. and Jim Gustafson were arrested for minor traffic violations without any threat to the safety of the arresting officer. Yet the officers were allowed to use the traffic arrest to conduct a complete body search of the arrestees to find evidence of still other crimes. The exterior of Arthur Lewis's automobile was searched and seized by the police though there was little, if any, danger that evidence might be destroyed if the police went to a judicial magistrate and obtained a search warrant. Arthur Lewis was already in custody and his car was going nowhere. A warrant could have been obtained within an hour. Yet this constitutional requirement was dispensed with and the officers searched and seized the automobile without a warrant. Chester Dombrowski was likewise in custody and his car was sitting in a privately owned garage. It was late at night, and again the gun that the police were looking for was certainly not a threat to anyone. A warrant to search the car could have been obtained. Again, the police thought it unnecessary and the Supreme Court's majority agreed. Eugene Edwards's clothes were stripped off his body some eight hours after his arrest to search for evidence against him. No danger was posed to officers' lives by the clothes and the evidence was apparently in no danger of being destroyed. After all, an eight-hour interlude was allowed to lapse before the clothes were seized and a warrant could have been obtained during that period of time. Again, the Fourth Amendment's requirements were obviated and the Supreme Court concurred.

It is easy to sympathize with the Burger court's efforts to dilute the Fourth Amendment since all cases coming before it readily evidence the guilt of the accused. There is little doubt in anyone's mind that Willie Robinson, Jr. or Jim Gustafson or Arthur Lewis or Chester Dombrowski or Eugene Edwards was, in fact, guilty of the crime as charged. Suppressing the evidence as illegally seized would certainly jeopardize the prosecution of the case at any retrial of the matter. Yet, in all cases before the Supreme Court involving the Fourth Amendment, the accused will probably be guilty as charged. The case only comes to the court on appeal after a jury has heard the evidence and returned a verdict of guilty. Where there is no guilt and an illegal search, the matter does not come to court in the course of a criminal prosecution. Yet, by loosening the constitutional standards on warrantless searches and seizures, the court makes inevitable police abuses as happened to Bill Pine and his family, Don and Virginia Askew, Herbert and Evelyn Giglotto, and countless others. In Fourth Amendment cases, the United States Supreme Court is not merely adjudicating the disposition of the case before it, but rather is also establishing the rules of procedure by which police searches and seizures can be effected. By diluting the requirement of pre-judicial screening of police searches, the Supreme Court is eliminating a historical screening device used to prevent the uncontrolled abuses of police power. If an officer had to sit down with a judge and explain why he wanted the search warrant, it seems improbable that the errors against the Askew and Giglotto families would have been committed. There still may be instances where a policeman might misread an address on a search warrant as in the case of Bill Pine, but such errors would be far less numerous than is susceptible in situations involving enthusiastic and warrantless searches of the wrong house. After all, the Fourth Amendment protects the innocent as well as the guilty, and it is unfortunate that the United States Supreme Court sets the rules of police search and seizure within the framework of insuring the conviction of the obviously guilty. Any case before the Supreme Court on searches and seizures involves not only protecting society by convicting the guilty but also insuring the privacy of all against uncontrolled executive power. By allowing the exception of searches incident to arrest to become the rule and thereby eliminate a pre-judicial screening of searches in such instances, society may well be further protected against criminals, but it is also less likely to be protected against its protectors. In a balance of society's rights against criminals and society's rights against uncontrolled police power, the Supreme Court has tilted the balance against criminals and against individual liberties. It is, of course, appropriate that criminals be punished for their illegal acts. It remains to be seen how many Pines, Askews, and Giglottos shall also be called upon to pay the price for such punishment.

Four:

Bail—
Preventive Detention
for the Poor

After arrest, the most pressing and immediate concern of the accused is getting out of police custody by posting bail. The procedure for implementing this universal desire of all charged with a crime is to take the suspect before a judicial magistrate where the accused is formally advised of the charges being brought against him while a preliminary determination as to the amount of bail is made. This procedure, called in many jurisdictions throughout the nation the preliminary arraignment, is short and simple. The defendant is handed a copy of the charges lodged against him, bail is set, a date for a preliminary hearing is indicated, and the accused is either released after bail is posted or committed to prison in default of bail. As a general rule, no lawyers are present. It is merely a matter of the arresting officer, the accused, and a magistrate. Yet, this step in the proceedings, which usually is completed in less than five minutes, is crucial in determining whether or not the accused will spend the time awaiting disposition of the charges inside of jail.

The option of the magistrate at the preliminary arraignment in the setting of bail is essentially threefold:

35

(1) set an exact monetary amount; (2) set nominal bail, usually $1.00; or (3) release the accused on his own recognizance (R-O-R), i.e., the defendant promises to pay a set amount if he fails to appear. The importance of this initial determination cannot be underestimated. Like most things in life, once bail is initially set, it is apt to follow the defendant in that same amount throughout the entire course of proceedings. It takes on a life of its own, and thereafter obtaining an increase—or decrease—is a rarity that requires initiative and powers of persuasion seldom found in the halls of criminal justice.

If bail is set in a specified monetary amount, and the accused and his family and friends are unable to raise it, the most novel and enterprising innovation of the criminal-law system then takes over: the bail bondsman. In simple terms, the bail bondsman is an insurance broker. He files a bond with the court insuring the accused's presence at all required court appearances. If the accused does not appear, the bail bondsman must pay to the court the full amount of the bail. In order for the defendant to secure the services of a bail bondsman, the accused must pay for his services. The general rule is that bail bondsmen require a ten percent premium of the full amount of the bail. In other words, if bail is set at $5,000, the accused must pay the bondsman $500. After being paid that amount, the bondsman puts up the entire $5,000 bond for the accused. If the defendant makes all the requisite court appearances, the bondsman gets his bail back. The accused, however, does not get back his premium. That money goes to the bondsman for services rendered. It can be a lucrative way of making a living.

The bail bondsman is under no obligation to accept a particular defendant as his client. Even if an accused has the money to buy a bondsman, he must first convince the bondsman that he can be counted on to appear at all mandated court appearances. If the bondsman believes that a particular defendant is a poor risk, he merely refuses to sell the accused his services. Furthermore, even after posting bail, a bondsman can change his mind. The bail bondsman merely secures the custody of the defendant, delivers the body of the accused to the proper authorities, and unilaterally advises them that he has changed his mind. Once the body of the accused has been placed into police custody, the bondsman has fulfilled his obligations to the court. In such circumstances, it is not at all clear whether the accused gets all, some, or none of his premium back. It is suspected that the practice in such instances where the bondsmen change their minds is anything but uniform.

In his most complex and socially rewarding roles, the bondsman is a surrogate policeman who performs a socially useful function for defendants, the courts, and the taxpayers. To defendants who cannot post their own bail but can afford the ten percent premium, a bondsman is a liberator. He keeps countless numbers of people out of jail while their cases are winding their way through the labyrinth of the criminal-law process. During this time while out on bail, the defendant can keep his job, be with his family, hire a lawyer, and prepare a defense. It is a lot easier to prepare for trial when the defendant is outside the jail walls and can assist his lawyer in securing witnesses whom the defense wishes to call. To the courts, the bail bondsman provides a semblance of order in the system of pretrial appearances by the accused. When a defendant fails to make a necessary court appearance, the court can issue a bench warrant for the absent offender and advise the bondsman that the bail he posted is being forfeited. This serves as an allurement to the bondsman to produce the body of the accused, no matter how belatedly. If the bondsman redelivers the suspect to police custody, the forfeiture is nullified, and the burden of recapturing prodigal defendants is lifted from the shoulders of the courts and the police. Furthermore, the bondsman is an independent set of eyes and ears in the community, often with more diverse contacts in the subculture of crime than available to the police. Ergo, the bail bondsman brings an entirely different perspective and enforcement mechanism for securing pretrial appearances by defendants than otherwise available to institutionalized law-enforcement officials. Finally, the bail bondsman provides a large service to the taxpayers. Instead of keeping presumably innocent defendants under lock and key at the expense of the taxpayers, and putting dependent families of the accused on the welfare roles, bondsmen allow the defendants to remain functioning within society until there is a final decision of their guilt or innocence. It is an indirect benefit at best, but in an era of overcrowded jails and ever-increasing costs of prison administration, the role of bondsmen in uncluttering our prisons with presumably innocent defendants is not an insignificant contribution. Of course, such noble motives scarcely appear on the mercenary gloss that ostensibly covers most bail bondsmen. In order to understand how the system functions, however, it is well to remember that bail bondsmen serve others as well as serving themselves.

After bail is set at the preliminary arraignment, the first court appearance delving into the factual basis of the arrest is the preliminary hearing. At the preliminary hearing, the prosecution must offer sufficient evidence to establish a *prima facie* case, i.e., indicate that the defendant probably committed a crime for which he ought to stand trial. Usually, the case at this stage of the proceeding is one-sided. The prosecution offers its evidence indicating guilt, and the defense presents no testimony whatsoever. In such circumstances, the only defense is on the quantum of proof; to wit, assuming that all the evidence offered by the prosecution is true, there is not sufficient evidence to indicate that the defendant is probably guilty of a crime. In this regard, it must be noted that, for purposes of establishing a *prima facie* case, there is an inarticulated presumption that the evidence offered by the prosecution is credible, and that the guilt of the accused must only be probable, not certain. Within this framework, the only substantive defense is an assertion of innocence. If the defendant at the preliminary hearing can prove to the satisfaction of the judge that he is, in fact, innocent, then obviously the prosecution has not established a *prima facie* case. Both instances are rare—failure by the prosecution to have sufficient evidence to indicate that the defendant is probably guilty, or an affirmative demonstration of innocence by the defense. The reason for this reality is that the law is structured at the level of the preliminary hearing to favor the prosecution, for the police as a rule do not arrest persons against whom there is no evidence of guilt. Once the judicial magistrate finds a *prima facie* case and sends the matter to the trial court for the ultimate determination of guilt, the focus of the law changes. Presumption of innocence. Guilt beyond a reasonable doubt. Such are the maxims that control at the trial of an accused. At the preliminary hearing, however, the standard is merely one of *prima facie* case or "probable guilt." Once this criterion has been satisfied, the matter is transferred to court and the accused must await formal court action.

After the preliminary hearing, the judicial magistrate will once again entertain either a prosecution or defense motion regarding bail. It is not uncommon, however, for the court to continue the terms and conditions of bail as previously set. If the facts of the case as brought out at the preliminary hearing are more heinous or gruesome than previously thought, the magistrate might very well increase the amount of bail. On the other hand, if the prosecution's case is weaker than expected and there appears the strong possibility that the defendant will be vindicated, the magistrate might very well be inclined to reduce bail. Such considerations, however, are really a perversion of the historic purpose of the system of bail. The only legitimate consideration in deciding the amount of bail is to insure the return of the accused for trial. Unfortunately, however, it is often a silent pretrial adjudication on the issue of guilt or innocence. Where the judicial magistrate believes guilt is assured, bail is high. Where guilt is in doubt, bail is low.

The most pervasive perversion in the setting of bail is in the establishment of a system of preventive detention. The concept of preventive detention is clearly contrary to our system that presumes that an accused is innocent until proven guilty. Preventive detention assumes that, not only is the accused guilty, but that if he is released on bail and allowed to roam the streets, he will commit still other unrelated crimes. Although the incidents of recidivism, i.e., repeated criminal behavior by the same people, and the realities of criminal law (many defendants steal in order to hire a lawyer) strongly suggest the possibility of still more crime by the same defendant, the concept of preventive detention cannot be reconciled with the Anglo-American heritage of due process of law before incarceration. Unfortunately, however, the setting of excessive bail has been used in order to insure that the accused will remain in custody pending disposition of the charges against him.

The greatest difficulty with the bail system is that there are no statutory norms for setting bail, and it is indeed doubtful whether or not any can be fashioned. The essence of the inquiry is subjective and the result to be attained is speculative. The precise question before each magistrate who is called to set bail is essentially an inquiry to decide how much money it will take to make sure that this defendant does indeed show up in court when required. Unfortunately, there is an unconscious presumption that favors the middle class when one of its members runs afoul of the law. Where one has no previous criminal record, is living in a traditional American family, has a steady job as a source of support, and has permanent roots in the community, the presumption is that one will appear in court even if guilty. It is the regularity and predictability of the middle-class life style that affords its members preferential treatment for purposes of setting bail. On the other hand, where one has had prior difficulties with the law, is not living in the basic family unit, is unemployed, and has no home and mortgage tying him to the community, the presumption is that, even if innocent, there is nothing to stop such a person from leaving the arm of the court. Such biases undoubtedly redound to the detriment of the lower class when bail is being set. It is not fair, for there are middle-class fugitives and lower-class defendants who are faithful to their word, but as George Bernard Shaw often observed, life is not fair, and there appears to be no legislative solution to remedy such inequities.

Within this entire framework, the greatest travesty of justice is the unconscious usage of bail as a system of preventive detention for the poor alone. In an affluent society, it is difficult to believe that there are persons who cannot scrape together $500 to post their own bail or to buy a bondsman for that $500 bail by giving him the necessary ten percent. There are people, however, who cannot meet bail no matter how reasonable the figure might appear to be to an outside observer, and they must whittle away their lives in jail, often on minor charges, waiting to be tried. To such persons, often the quickest way out of jail is to plead guilty to the offense because the time served in jail is already greater than the anticipated sentence of the court. It is difficult for an affluent America to empathize with the plight of the poor who congest the jails prior to trial because they cannot post bail or afford the bail bondsman. The tragedy is so far removed from the life styles of most that it cannot be comprehended even when brought out into the open. But it is rarely a topic of discussion, for these wretches of humanity are locked behind bars and are out of the sight or hearing of most of us. It is a sad commentary on our system of bail to insure presence at trial, but for now, there appears no other way. The only redress for such defendants is a truly speedy trial so their guilt or innocence can be quickly adjudicated. A system of priority for offenders in jail on minor offenses might be the only answer so such defendants are not placed in the position of pleading guilty in order to be free. Such persons are, however, the weak, the powerless, the unglamorous, and they escape the attention of the media and the criminal justice administrators. A former United States attorney general, William Saxbe, has called for the speedy trial of the alleged perpetrators of violent crime so justice for them can be quick and vengeful. Such proposals only victimize the unglamorous defendants whose crimes are minor but whose detention in prison is real. Until the constitutional ideal of speedy trial for all is a reality, the bail system and preventive detention for the poor are realities that must be ignobly endured by a proud nation.

Five:

Defining Crime—
The Failure to Define

One major purpose of criminal statutes is to deter individuals from engaging in certain proscribed forms of human behavior. Criminal statutes that describe criminal behavior, therefore, are generally considered to place strictures on human activity by limiting the type of conduct in which persons can engage. This perception of criminal law, however, is inaccurate. Criminal statutes prohibit *nothing*. Instead, the statutes are drafted to punish *past* behavior and are applied in factual situations that are a *fait accompli*. In short, criminal law punishes the murderer after the victim is dead. It does not prohibit the murder of the victim. It cannot stop the homicide. It merely punishes the perpetrator of the death after it is successfully accomplished. The deterrent effect, if any, comes from the knowledge on the part of the perpetrator of the death that he is liable to be punished if he is discovered, captured, and convicted. It is essential in understanding the criminal adjudicatory system to realize that the legislative standards of criminal behavior apply to completed human conduct, not potential human action, and that crime is simply what the legislature says it is.

In defining crime, legislatures have traditionally used broad and comprehensive categories of obnoxious human behavior and applied different standards of punishment to the various divisions of outlawed conduct. Generally, the crimes are of three species: (1) offenses against the person, (2) offenses against property, and (3) offenses against the body politic or offenses against society. There are, of course, no clear lines of demarcation among the three and there is, of necessity, a certain amount of overlap among them. By way of example, homicide, robbery, rape, kidnapping, and assault are the clearest illustrations of offenses against the person. Murder is, of course, also a crime against the body politic and very often it is done for pecuniary motives. The individual who is murdered, however, is primarily the aggrieved party, and the heart of the crime is the spilling of human blood. For these reasons, murder is generally regarded as an offense against the person. Similarly, robbery invariably involves the forceful taking of property by one person from another human being. The baseness of the offense, however, rests not in the taking of the property but rather in the threat or usage of force against a fellow human being in acccomplishing the objective. For this reason, robbery, armed or unarmed, also qualifies as an offense against the person. Assaults on the person, rape, and kidnapping are, of course, obvious violations of the dignity of a human being.

Offenses against property are more numerous and multifaceted. Theft. Arson. Embezzlement. Fraudulent conversion of property. Burglary. Forgery. Criminal trespass. The component parts of each offense vary, but all possess a common element: the appropriation of another's property for the perpetrator's use, or the destruction of another's property so the owner is deprived of the benefit of his possession.

Offenses against the body politic enjoy no common element. The crimes against society are as varied as the diverse and often conflicting interests of the body politic itself. Perjury. Prostitution. Drug possession and trafficking. Drunken driving. Bribery. Gambling. Bigamy. Incest. The list is endless. The only test for determining the purpose of criminality of the offense against society is by ascertaining the cultural milieu that fosters the value that the behavior offends. A society that values truthfulness under oath stipulates that lying under oath is a crime. A society that believes in sexual exclusivity in marriage arrests prostitutes. A society that idolizes rationality condemns the usage and selling of drugs. A society that depends on the automobile for transportation cannot afford to allow drunken persons to drive. A society that believes in the work ethic cannot chance wealth and riches to the vagaries of fate and gambling. A society that is premised on the family and monogamy cannot tolerate polygamy or incest. The norms of society determine how individuals who forsake the normal shall be punished. Such is the variety in the usage of criminal statutes to punish offenses against the body politic.

The initial difficulty rests in determining the appropriateness of labeling certain human behavior criminal. Assuming that can be done with a general consensus of rationality free from whim and caprice, the real problem is defining criminal activity with the requisite degree of precision. In theory, murder is the most heinous of all crimes, and, traditionally, it has been punished most severely. It does not take an observer of criminal justice long, however, to realize that murderers are, as a rule, the most pathetic and least dangerous of all types of criminal personalities. The person who murders usually acts out of momentary anger, haste, and rashness. The murderer usually murders a relative, a friend, or an acquaintance, and almost always feels true contrition for the act. There are, as always, exceptions. There are murderers who kill for fun, for sex, or for profit. But as a rule, murderers are not "bad" people. They are not inherently evil. They probably have never been arrested before for any crime whatsoever. Yet these are the people who are usually punished most severely, and in most cases, they are the least in need of rehabilitation.

Compare the average murderer to the armed robber. The armed robber is the most vicious and dangerous of all criminals. The robber takes a gun, or a knife, or whatever, and threatens to take a human life in order to steal tangible personal property, and he probably will keep functioning until he gets caught. Yet the armed robber does not inspire the traditional antipathy that the murderer does, and he will probably be out on the street again doing the same old thing long before the contrite murderer who is least apt to repeat his crime. The example may be extreme, but it is nevertheless accurate, and until there is a realistic categorization of crime, the criminal system will continue locking up the wrong people for the longer periods of time, and the dangerous criminal types will be free to roam the streets almost at will.

The point of the overstated example is that murder must be subcategorized, and that the traditional first- and second-degree, voluntary- and involuntary-manslaughter definitions simply do not work. A man who gets into a savage fight with his irascible mother-in-law, walks into the next room to get his revolver out of his desk, loads the gun with six bullets, and returns to put six slugs into her is probably guilty of first-degree murder. He should not, however, be treated the same as the paid assassin, the pervert who kills for fun, the sex killer, the kidnapper who executes the victim, or the armed robber who murders during the course of still another crime. Yet he is, and that is why the criminal-law system does not work.

Another illustration of the failure to properly subdivide and categorize crime is the prosecution of the apprehended kidnapper. In most states, the kidnapper who frees his victim is treated the same for purposes of trial for kidnapping as the kidnapper who murders his helpless hostage. Furthermore, the kidnapper of a child for ransom is regarded the equal of the runaway felon who forces his way into an adult's automobile and drives away in the car with the adult in tow. By subdividing the crime of kidnapping into its various types, a more realistic definition of the crime can be achieved. Kidnapping a child subsequently freed. Kidnapping an adult subsequently freed. Kidnapping a child subsequently freed but molested while a hostage. Kidnapping a child who accidentally dies during the kidnap. Kidnapping a child who is subsequently freed by the police. Kidnapping a hostage during the course of a crime. Such categories immediately come to mind. The list is not definitive. It illustrates, however, the variants of kidnapping that ought to be treated by statute in order to establish a more realistic code of crime.

Murder and kidnapping are only two examples. The same categorization can be done with all traditional crimes. Instead of using broad generalized categories to define crime, specific forms of the same odious generic conduct ought to be spelled out in order to allow different and more precise forms of punishment. Historically, legislators have drafted criminal statutes in simple comprehensive terms in order to limit loopholes and make the task of prosecution easier. To understand this concern, it must be remembered that it is an axiom of criminal law that the prosecution must prove beyond a reasonable doubt each and every element of the offense. For example, burglary at nighttime became difficult to prove because the prosecution often could not establish with the requisite degree of specificity the time of the offense. Consequently, failure to prove that the burglary occurred at nighttime jeopardized the entire prosecution, even though there was no real doubt that the defendant had, in fact, burglarized a dwelling as charged. To limit such a result, legislators remedied the problem by reducing criminal activity to its barest elements. The unfortunate by-product of this short-cut was to lump together dissimilar criminality into the same category. To illustrate this point, the burglary example is still helpful. Generally, burglary is defined in terms of an unlawful entering of a building, dwelling, or structure with the intent to commit a crime therein (usually, though not necessarily, theft). Consequently, a professional burglar who enters into a home at night with the intent to steal, but who is probably prepared to kill if the residents should discover him, is guilty of burglary. So, also, is the eighteen-year-old lad who enters an unoccupied record store late at night to steal a few records. Then, again, so is the farmer who breaks into his neighbor's barn and takes out a few bales of hay while the neighbor is vacationing. The same holds true for the rambunctious teen-agers who re-enter their school building in the dark of night and vandalize the classrooms. Under the broad concept of burglary, all are guilty of the same crime, but it hardly seems fair or desirable to equate the professional cat burglar's crime with that of unruly school children who vandalize a school or with the farmer who steals some hay.

The task confronting the legislators of today is to determine on the part of their constituents the specific conduct that needs to be outlawed and to establish a rational grading system of crime based upon actual conduct rather than upon imaginary grades of the same offense.

Unfortunately, the new trend favors less specificity as evidenced by the new Model Penal Code that propounds a system of criminal offenses labeled felony 1, 2, or 3, or misdemeanor 1, 2, or 3. Consequently, the new code that is being adopted by more and more states uses the same broad or even broader categories to address specific forms of repulsive conduct. Such categorization, therefore, becomes artificial and serves no useful purpose in grading the reprehensibleness of particular criminal actions.

If more specificity in defining crime is to be used, the problem of limiting loopholes and not needlessly multiplying the elements of the offense still remains. In order to accomplish the objective of requisite specificity without creating cumbersome technicalities, an innovative usage of the concept of "lesser included offenses" must come into widespread use. To illustrate the application of the notion of lesser included offense, it is best to proceed by example. Aggravated assault generally refers to an unlawful striking or hitting that causes serious bodily injury. On the other hand, simple assault usually embraces an unlawful hitting or touching without serious injury. The question that a jury must decide in an aggravated assault prosecution is the extent of the injury as developed by the evidence. Where aggravated assault is charged but the jury believes that there was a striking without the requisite degree of injury, the concept of lesser included offense allows the jury to return a verdict of guilty to simple assault only because the jury believes that all the elements of the offense were present *except* the required degree of bodily injury. By using this same technique, the problem of specific offenses without technical difficulties can be obviated.

Essentially, each offense would retain a generic definition of the crime that would be retained as a criminal violation. Aggravating—or mitigating—elements would then be added as a subdivision of the generic offense as separate and distinct criminal statutes. To illustrate the operation of this proposal, the burglary situation is useful. Burglary would be retained as the unauthorized entrance into a building or structure with the intent to commit a crime therein. There would also be, however, separate indictable offenses of burglary at nighttime, burglary of a private residence, burglary of an occupied private residence, burglary at nighttime of a private residence, burglary at nighttime of an occupied private residence, burglary of a commercial dwelling containing movable property in excess of $100,000, burglary at nighttime of a commercial dwelling containing property in excess of $100,000, burglary of an occupied commercial dwelling containing property in excess of $100,000, burglary at nighttime of an occupied commercial dwelling containing property in excess of $100,000. The list is not definitive, but it serves to indicate the types of burglary that might reasonably be considered to be more serious than merely entrance into a building to commit a crime. Likewise, mitigating circumstances would also be built into the statutory scheme. Burglary by a person less than twenty-five years of age. Burglary of an unoccupied structure left unattended. Burglary of an unoccupied structure left unattended and by a person less than twenty-five years of age. Burglary by a person apprehended at the scene without a weapon. Burglary of an unoccupied structure left unattended and by a person less than twenty-five years of age and apprehended at the scene without a weapon. Again, the list is not comprehensive, but it does indicate the types of burglary that might be considered less serious than usually associated with the crime of burglary.

Under the proposed system, a person charged with a crime would always face the generic violation and, additionally, either the aggravating or mitigating variants as the evidence preliminarily indicates. Of course, conviction could only result under one of the charges, and that would be determined by the facts as found by the jury. In this manner, statutory standards of criminal behavior would more accurately reflect the actual activities that criminal statutes attempt to punish and a finding of guilt would be a more realistic appraisal of the culpability of the transgressor. If the criminal-law system is to deal more justly and effectively with its prodigal sons, then the base from which it works—the definition of crime—must be exact. Scrupulous adherence to the actuality of criminal conduct instead of generalized definitions of criminal conduct must be the framework upon which the criminal-justice system is founded. The present system is remiss in its failure to define the details of crime. Only through a substantial revision of our present statutory system can this deficiency be eliminated.

Six:

Pretrial Motions—
The Real Battle

Prior to the actual trial of a case, defense counsel must plan his strategy. An integral part of such strategy is using pretrial motions to determine just how much evidence the prosecution has and how much of that evidence will be used at the trial. For it is an axiom of criminal law that the jury never hears all the evidence that the police may have against a defendant and that all evidence must be sifted by the rules of evidence and the rules of criminal procedure.

The avowed purpose of the rules of evidence is to insure fairness to the defendant by allowing only evidence that meets the historical test of reliability. For example, the hearsay rule is a rule of evidence that holds that any out-of-court statement offered for the truth of its content is generally inadmissible in the trial of the case. In other words, a witness cannot take the stand to testify that he was told by Mary Jones that she saw Paul Smith, the defendant, commit the crime. Since Mary Jones viewed the crime, only she can testify as to what she saw. Persons in whom she confides do not become witnesses against the defendant merely because Mary Jones told them what she observed. The basis for such a rule is the reliability of information test. Anglo-American law has frowned upon another-person-told-me stories as not worthy of belief, and therefore inadmissible in a court of law. The rules of criminal procedure, however, also exclude evidence not because of unreliability but on other policy grounds. As such, the rules of criminal procedure are far more important in structuring the trial and are less likely to be related to serving the process of truth.

The most significant rule of criminal procedure is the "exclusionary rule." In *Weeks* v. *United States,* 232 U.S. 383, 34 S.Ct. 341, 58 L.Ed. 652 (1916), Fremont Weeks was convicted in federal court for illegally using the mails to transport lottery tickets. The evidence used against him was seized from his house by federal agents without his consent and without the use of a search warrant. On appeal, the United States Supreme Court held that the evidence was seized in violation of the warrant requirement of the Fourth Amendment, and that it must, therefore, be excluded from use in evidence against Weeks.

In *Wolf* v. *Colorado,* 338 U.S. 25, 69 S.Ct. 1359, 93 L. Ed. 1782 (1949), the United States Supreme Court was confronted with an issue similar to that in the Weeks case. Evidence was admittedly seized from Jenkin Wolf without a warrant and was thereafter introduced into evidence against him. Unlike the *Weeks* case, however, the evidence was seized by state law enforcement personnel, not federal agents, and Wolf was convicted in state court, not federal court. In an opinion by Justice Frankfurter thirty-five years after the application of the exclusionary rule in the *Weeks* case, the United States Supreme Court held that although illegally seized evidence is not admissible in a federal forum, it is admissible in a state trial because the exclusionary rule was not mandated by the Constitution.

In simple terms, the status of the law in 1949 was that all illegal searches and seizures were prohibited by the United States Constitution but that the Constitution did not demand that illegally seized evidence be inadmissible in a court of law. The federal courts had decided in 1914 by virtue of the *Weeks* decision that it would on policy grounds exclude such evidence from trials before the federal tribunals. The express policy behind such exclusion was that federal agents would not illegally seize evidence if they could not use it at trial, and the constitutional protection against unreasonable searches and seizures would thereby be effectuated. There was, however, no constitutional imperative that state courts adopt that same policy in order to deter illegal searches and seizures by its policemen.

Admittedly, there are other remedies available to protect the guarantee of freedom from illegal searches and seizures. Fines and suspensions of policemen who engage in such conduct are probably a more efficient remedy. For a repeated offender, being fired from the police force could be the ultimate in punishment. Furthermore, in support of such alternate protection, it is argued that illegally seized evidence is no less reliable than legally seized evidence, so the jury would not be misled by its introduction into evidence. As a practical matter, however, law-enforcement personnel were not being fired for over-enthusiasm in performing illegal searches and seizures. If the constitutional guarantee of freedom from unreasonable searches and seizures was to be meaningful, the United States Supreme Court decided in 1914 that the illegally seized evidence must be excluded from the trial, irrespective of its relevance, reliability, and materiality. In 1949, however, the United States Supreme Court refused to apply this same rule of law to the states.

The combined impact of *Weeks* and *Wolf* was minimal. Federal officials could not use illegally seized evidence, but state officials could. The bulk of criminal law work has always been conducted in the state forums. It is no exaggeration to estimate that well over ninety percent of all criminal prosecutions in the United States are a matter of state law. Within this context, the limited scope of the exclusionary rule must be understood throughout the first half of the twentieth century.

During the first half of the twentieth century, Justice Frankfurter also wrote an opinion where he used a descriptive metaphor to describe the exclusionary rule, to wit, the "fruit of the poisonous tree" analogy. In *Nardone* v. *United States*, 308 U.S. 338, 69 S.Ct. 266, 844 L.Ed. 307 (1939), Frank Nardone had his original conviction overturned because evidence used against him at his trial came from an illegal wiretap. At his second trial, the prosecution again offered similar evidence to that obtained from the illegal wiretap, and Nardone contended that this information was only available to the prosecution because it had the benefit of the information from the illegal wiretap. The trial court refused to allow defense counsel to explore the manner in which the prosecution obtained the distilled information, and the matter was appealed to the United States Supreme Court. On appeal, the court again reversed the conviction and remanded it back to the trial court to determine whether or not the information in the second trial was also premised in the illegal wiretap. The logic of the rule was that not only illegally seized evidence cannot be used *at trial*, but further that it cannot be used *at all*, even for the purpose of uncovering other evidence. In so holding, Justice Frankfurter penned his "fruit of the poisonous tree" metaphor, that is, just like fruit from a poisonous tree is not edible, evidence that is premised in illegal police activity cannot be used in any fashion whatsoever.

The "fruit of the poisonous tree" doctrine was a further expansion of the concept of the exclusionary rule. As originally applied, the exclusionary rule only limited the use of the illegally seized evidence at trial. With the "fruit of the poisonous tree" rationale, however, the evidence and the mere knowledge of its existence also became taboo. For example, assume that the police illegally seized corporate books and documents during an investigation. Thereafter, the defendant obtains a court order requiring the police to return such documents to his possession. The police then attempt to obtain a search warrant to examine the books and documents, and use as their basis for requesting the warrant the fact that they had seen such evidence with their own eyes while it was illegally in police custody. Under the "fruit of the poisonous tree" doctrine, such knowledge of the existence of the records is tainted by the original police illegality and cannot, therefore, be used as a basis for obtaining a valid search warrant.

The "fruit of the poisonous tree" doctrine had little impact on the administration of criminal law in the first half of the twentieth century inasmuch as the concept of excluding evidence still remained only a matter of federal law. State prosecutors were, therefore, still constitutionally free to use the illegally seized evidence at trial and for whatever other investigatory purpose they had. The stage was set, however, for the widespread exclusion of evidence and the benefit of knowing its existence by Justice Frankfurter's poisoned-tree rationale.

In *Mapp* v. *Ohio*, 367 U.S. 643, 81 S.Ct. 1684, 6 L.Ed. 2d 1081 (1961), Dollree Mapp was convicted under Ohio law for the possession and control of certain lascivious books, pictures, and photographs. Such items were seized in Mrs. Mapp's home after an extensive search, without the benefit of a search warrant, of her premises from the basement up to and including her young daughter's bedroom. Under existing law as defined by *Wolf* v. *Colorado, supra,* such evidence, though illegally seized, was properly admitted into evidence because the officers were Cleveland policemen and the prosecution was under state law. On appeal to the United States Supreme Court where the parties vigorously argued the constitutionality of the state obscenity statute, the Supreme Court used the case to decide that illegally seized evidence could no longer be used in state prosecution and thereby extended the exclusionary rule of *Weeks* v. *United States, supra,* to the state forum.

The *Mapp* case, combined with Justice Frankfurter's "fruit of the poisonous tree" principle of law, marked the beginnings of the criminal-law revolution of the Warren Court. Once the exclusionary rule was applied to the state court systems, where the bulk of criminal-law prosecutions take place, and once this principle of excluding evidence was interpreted as holding that, if the police make a mistake in criminal procedure—even *good faith* errors regarding legal technicalities—the evidence was poisoned, the focus of criminal defense then became centered on such technicalities with the view toward preventing the jury from seeing or hearing good, sound, reliable evidence. Pretrial motions, therefore, become the forum where the underlying issue of guilt or innocence is litigated, for by deciding preliminarily what facts the jury ultimately will or will not hear, the courts set up the legal framework of the trial. In essence, then, the courts are deciding what the jury will hear and what evidence the jurors can consider in their deliberations. As in the case of Dollree Mapp, the jury could hardly convict her for possession of obscene literature if the jury could not see the allegedly obscene material. In such instances where the actual evidence of the crime itself is no longer admissible, the prosecution has no option but to drop the charges. In other cases, prosecution might be jeopardized, but still possible. For example, if the court held in a murder prosecution that the gun with the defendant's fingerprints could not be introduced into evidence, the prosecution might still be able to prove its case by other extrinsic evidence. The use of the weapon laden with the perpetrator's fingerprints, however, would surely assist the prosecution. Its exclusion from evidence would not be a necessarily fatal blow to prosecution.

Once the exclusion-of-evidence rule became an accepted legal principle in the administration of criminal law in state forums, it only naturally followed that it would be extended into areas of law other than suppressing physical evidence seized in legal searches. In *Miranda* v. *Arizona*, 384 U.S. 436, 86 S.Ct. 1602, 16 L.Ed. 2d 694 (1966), Ernesto A. Miranda was taken to police headquarters, sequestered from family and friends, interrogated for hours, and finally confessed to kidnapping and rape. There was no contention that physical threats or abuse induced the confession. On the contrary, Chief Justice Warren stated unequivocally that the duress involved, if any, was only psychological. Furthermore, the Chief Justice observed that, under traditional rules of evidence, the confession would probably be considered voluntary. Nevertheless, the United States Supreme Court concluded that any confession given without the defendant first being advised of his right to remain silent and his right to his own or a court-appointed lawyer during the custodial interrogation shall be presumed to be coerced. Furthermore, the Supreme Court went on to conclude that such "coerced" confessions shall be excluded from evidence regardless of their relevancy, reliability, or materiality.

In *United States* v. *Wade*, 388 U.S. 218, 87 S.Ct. 1926, 18 L.Ed. 2d 1149 (1967), Billie Joe Wade was convicted of bank robbery. The heart of the case against him was the positive identification of Billie Joe as the robber by two of the bank tellers. Prior to the trial, Billie Joe Wade was placed in a line-up of five or six other persons, and picked out of the line-up by both tellers. Although Wade was represented by a lawyer at the time of the line-up, the fact of the impending line-up was not communicated to his lawyer.

At the trial, Wade's lawyer argued that conducting a line-up without the presence of the accused's lawyer violates his right to effective assistance of counsel because the lawyer would be unaware of any prejudicial taint occurring during the line-up by the structuring of the line-up. For example, where the victim of a robbery identifies the perpetrator as an Oriental, the police have been known to use one Oriental and all other Occidentals in the line-up. Where the accused is identified as a youth under twenty, police have composed the line-up of one youth and five other persons well over forty. Such suggestions regarding the identity of the accused can be so prejudicial that a lawyer's presence is necessary to protect the accused from unfair bias against him.

In the *Wade* case, the United States Supreme Court accepted the premise that a line-up without the assistance of counsel might be unfair. The Supreme Court, however, was reluctant to adopt a blanket rule and hold that, once a line-up without the assistance of counsel is conducted, no further identification can be made of the accused by the victims at the trial of the case. Instead, the court held that a pretrial hearing must be held to determine whether or not the victims can still identify the accused based upon the original observation and without the benefit of the illegal line-up. If an independent basis of identification can be demonstrated, the accused may still be identified by the victims at the trial of the case despite the illegal line-up. If no such independent origin of identification can be shown and the line-up was illegally conducted, then the identification of the accused by witnesses who attended the line-up must be suppressed.

Suppression of the physical evidence of the crime. Suppression of the accused's confession. Suppression of eyewitness testimony identifying the accused as the perpetrator of the crime. Such pretrial factors undoubtedly affect the jury's ultimate decision. If the burglar tools seized from the defendant's person are not admitted into evidence, it may be difficult to convince the jury that the accused burglarized a particular building. If the accused's confession is not brought out at the trial, the jury might not believe the circumstantial evidence indicating guilt. If the rape victim is not allowed to identify the man who attacked her because she attended a line-up where the accused was not represented by counsel, it is impossible to convict the rapist. The exclusionary rule is not designed to serve the process of fact-finding before the jury. On the contrary, its purpose is to hide facts from the jury in order that other, more important constitutional policies might be served.

In suppressing illegally seized evidence, the avowed purpose is to require police officers to obey the constitutional requirement of reasonable searches and seizures, or else their efforts at crime detection will be in vain. In suppressing confessions where the accused was not given the opportunity to confer with counsel, the reason is to insure that the police advise all defendants of their constitutional right to effective assistance of counsel. In suppressing an eyewitness identification where there was an illegal line-up, again the rationale is to require policemen to refrain from circumventing an accused's right to counsel. In the line-up instance, the Supreme Court did intertwine the issue with the reliability of the evidence and the possibility of prejudicial taint accompanying the line-up. By adopting the exclusionary rule, however, where there is no independent origin of identification, the court succumbed to its propensity to exclude evidence that the jury as the trier of facts ought to be hearing.

The constitutional policies behind the suppression concept are important. Police ought to be limited only to reasonable searches and seizures. Defendants deserve to be represented by lawyers at all stages of a criminal prosecution, including custodial interrogation. Line-ups must be conducted fairly if the innocent are to be protected from errors in police work. It remains, however, an established fact that suppression of evidence does little to serve such laudable constitutional objectives and other mechanisms must be found to protect the innocent, prosecute the guilty, and implement our system of constitutional rights. The countless number of reported cases where courts have suppressed evidence because of good-faith errors on the part of the police are testimony to the fact that the suppression rule is not an adequate mechanism for deterring police misconduct. On the other hand, suppression of such reliable evidence is hardly in keeping with the premise of Anglo-American law that truth and justice are best served by allowing competing adversaries to present their cases to the jury for its determination on all the facts.

If police misconduct is the culprit, then the laudable constitutional objectives can be served by replacing the exclusionary rule with a statutory system of graduated punishment for the offending officer. It does not seem unrealistic to establish a system where an individual police officer is allowed one good-faith error a year. After the first error, then there ought to be a scale of graduated punishment including fines and suspensions with termination of employment as the final penalty. Such a statutory procedure would more effectively induce police diligence in respecting our system of constitutional guarantees than the mere exclusion of evidence. Furthermore, in order to insure that policemen would not risk personal punishment in order to "get" particular individuals, the exclusionary rule might still be applied in those instances where the police error was either intentional or malicious. Under such a system, legal technicalities in criminal law would be placed in a more realistic perspective and equal justice under law might become an actualized ideal.

In the present climate of criminal law, the evenhanded administration of justice is no longer even a fanciful dream. Two persons engaged in the exact same type of criminality can be treated entirely different depending upon the competency of the arresting officers. If the first offender is arrested by a highly efficient and scrupulously diligent policeman, and the second by a blundering patrolman who muddles through, the first is apt to be convicted while the second is released for the violation of his constitutional rights. Such disparity in result cannot be tolerated if equal justice under the law is to be served.

There was a time in Anglo-American civil law when exactitude in the presentation of the case was required if relief was to be obtained from the courts. Common-law pleadings, however, have fallen into disfavor, and the courts no longer tell civil litigants that one error dooms forever the case. While this fascination with exactitude has been eliminated in civil law, the trend in criminal justice has been one of absolute intolerance of any police errors whatsoever. This attitude is highly unrealistic, for it must be remembered that police forces are peopled with mere mortal men. In a democratic society, it is necessary that police authority be scrutinized and controlled. The exclusionary rule for good-faith errors, however, is not the proper means of reviewing and punishing police misconduct. Graduated punishment aimed at the offending officers and the use of the exclusionary rule only for intentional or malicious police behavior is an alternative that can effect truth and justice at individual trials while at the same time affirmatively promoting our constitutional guarantees.

Seven:

Victimless Crime—
Chipmunks, Chipmunks,
Chipmunks

There is a true story famous in Pennsylvania legal circles about an unabashed Philadelphia judge who was notorious for telling everyone what was on his mind. One particular day when the judge was feeling not even the slightest of judicial inhibitions, he strode up to the bench only to be presented by an assistant district attorney with a long list of cases to be heard that day. As he surveyed the caseload, he found to his amazement that all of the offenses involved number runners, prostitutes, homosexuals, junkies, and other such nonviolent offenders. In a curt bluster of judicial flurry, the judge summed up the paradox of prosecuting victimless crime. "Chipmunks, chipmunks, chipmunks," he roared in unqualified disgust. "Philadelphia is crawling with wolves, and all you bring me are chipmunks. Cases dismissed."

The categories of victimless crime are varied and numerous. Prostitution. Sodomy or "deviate" sexual intercourse. Pornography. Drug possession. Drug trafficking. Gambling. Adultery. Fornication. Drunkenness. All jurisdictions in various degrees define as criminal species of the aforementioned activities. The particular statutory offenses vary by definition, but all are an attempt to prohibit variants of such behavior. Yet no unwilling parties are victims, and the victims, if any, are the people who voluntarily engage in such activities.

It is far too simplistic to point out that there are no victims of prostitution, sodomy, pornography, drug possession and trafficking, gambling, adultery, fornication, and drunkenness. The prostitute and her pimp, the drug user and his supplier, the gambler, and the drunk present social problems. Prostitutes spread venereal disease. Smut peddlers debase commercial neighborhoods. Heavy drug users victimize themselves. Ardent gamblers will take the food from the mouths of children to play a horse, or spin the wheel, or be dealt another hand of cards. Such people are problems to themselves and to all the people who are near them. The real question is whether or not the criminal-law system is the mechanism for correcting such maladies.

Early in this century, a group of determined activists recognized the problems caused by liquor and attempted to rectify the matter by the absolute prohibition on the manufacture and sale of liquor in the United States. This misdirected effort at solving the problems associated with alcohol only compounded the evils. Instead of legal corporate entities reaping profits from the production of liquor, illegal noncorporate alliances formed to make fortunes in satisfying the unquenchable thirst for alcohol. Instead of quality control of liquor by reputable producers, ambitious and greedy knaves made and sold drinks that blinded, crippled, and killed. Instead of halting the sale of liquor, an outlaw subculture grew up and prospered by selling illegal beverages.

It is not uncommon to hear old judges, who, in their youth, frequented speakeasies, lecture young defendants on the evils of marijuana. One is almost tempted to rebuke such robed men and recall for such judges their less than straight-and-narrow path when they, too, acted outside the law. Such an effort, however, would be in vain. Alcohol is not marijuana, and to such eyes that is all the difference that is required. Yet alcohol remains today as much a problem as it was in pre-Prohibition time. Alcoholics victimize themselves, their families, their employers and often commit other unrelated crimes. As the casual observer of the criminal-law system quickly learns, there is a correlation between drinking and crimes involving assaults. More than one arson, assault, or murder has been precipitated in a mind awash with liquor. Yet there is almost universal agreement that a return to prohibition is not the answer.

Society and the law have come to accommodate themselves to the use of alcoholic beverages. The accommodation has taken the form of creating vast regulatory agencies that oversee the manufacture, distribution, and sale of alcoholic beverages, and prescribe the terms and conditions of doing business. The problems of alcoholism remain. The problems of liquored-up troublemakers are still all too evident in the criminal courts of this nation. Yet society attempts to cope with the residual effects of alcohol consumption by other, noncriminal ways. Alcoholics Anonymous is an exemplary tribute to the usage of nongovernmental resources to treat the problems of liquor. The law for its part does not generally allow one to excuse criminal behavior because liquor was the motivating factor. In this manner, society responds to the problems of alcohol, and the law warns those who drink to excess that they will not curry favor in the criminal law forum for their failure to learn moderation. But more importantly, society has come to learn that the power of criminal law is indeed limited and that all problems involving distasteful human behavior cannot be solved. In the final analysis, if an individual chooses to destroy himself with drink, society and the law must stand by and let him.

Cigarette smoking is another illustration of society's willingness to accommodate itself to known dangers. According to medical experts, smoking causes lung cancer. There is also a correlation between smoking and other nonrespiratory diseases, including heart attacks. The scientific evidence that cigarette smoking is dangerous to health is far more extensive and conclusive than the evidence on the alleged danger of marijuana smoking. Yet criminal law does not outlaw cigarette smoking, and there is no widespread clamor to save cigarette smokers from themselves. Society and the law have reached an accommodation with cigarettes, and the smokers who succumb to their evils are treated humanely in hospitals and buried with distinction when medical science cannot save their lives.

Perhaps the time has come for society and the law to reach a similar accommodation with prostitutes and their pimps, with the purveyors of smut and their customers, with the drug user and his supplier, with the gambler and the sodomist and other nonviolent offenders of the sensibilities of others. Regulation may be part of the answer. Prostitution licenses and concomitant periodic medical checkups might be necessary to· battle venereal disease. Government-run or government-licensed casinos might be a necessity if the gambler is to get at least an honest deal. Zoning restrictions might be required to keep the smut peddlers from driving out established commercial entities and instead bringing in other such merchants. Governmental assistance for the addict who sees the error of his way and wants to break the habit might be the only feasible way to help those who want to help themselves. Regulation, however, will not eliminate the problems. The remaining part of the accommodation will necessitate an understanding that all the problems associated with prostitution, sodomy, pornography, drug possession and trafficking, gambling, and drunkenness cannot be solved. In the final analysis, if a person insists on shooting heroin into his veins until it kills him, society and the law must stand idly by and allow it to happen. If a girl wants to give up her youth by offering $20 screws, society and the law must restrain themselves and allow her the freedom of choice. If a man wants to risk venereal disease by cavorting with ladies of the night, society and the law must realize that it is his choice. If a gambler spends his life and a small fortune chasing after a bigger and instantaneous fortune, the freedom to dream—and err—must remain with the individual. The law must assume a position of benign neglect to the self-made victims of victimless crime. They cannot be helped, and the law can merely function to institutionalize by regulation previously unlawful behavior into an atmosphere where its reach is limited and confined.

Throughout the debate on the efficacy of statutes creating victimless crime, there has been constant reference to the question of the ability of legislatures to legislate morality. The question so posed is more academic than real. Anglo-American law has, in certain instances, quite successfully legislated morality. For example, the prohibition of bigamy and polygamy and instead our system of staggered monogamy, i.e., you can have more than one spouse, but only one spouse at a time, is a successful effort at legislating morality. The success in applying this restriction by law, however, depends almost wholeheartedly on the near-universal acceptance by all members of society that monogamy is the way it ought to be. In other words, the law works not because it is the law but rather it is the law because that is what the people believe.

Within such a narrow context, legislators can successfully legislate morality, which is really nothing more than reinforcing the moral code that the society itself embraces. When acceptance of moral principles regarding prostitution, homosexuality, drug use, alcohol, pornography, and gambling is something less than near-universal, however, constant breaches and challenges to the codification of morals become inevitable. Hence, the situation arises where a Philadelphia judge could walk into a courtroom filled with number runners, prostitutes, homosexuals, and junkies and other drug users. The significant question becomes, therefore, not whether legislators can legislate morality, but what happens if legislators fail to legislate morality.

There is a positive correlation between violent crime and drug offenders. Junkies rob in order to put heroin into their veins. It is not uncommon for prostitutes to set up their patrons for mugging and robbery. Desperate gamblers have felt an overriding compulsion to steal when their debits exceed their credits. The difficulty lies in attempting to predict what will happen if the criminal-law strictures on prostitution, sodomy, pornography, drug possession and trafficking, gambling, and drunkenness are removed and instead replaced with mere governmental regulation. Will the subcultures of crime fostered and promoted by years of outlaw status continue to flourish in the open once the threat of criminal punishment is removed? There are no hard empirical data by which one can predict the future. Fortunately, however, there is some historical precedent that should be borne in mind when attempting to uncover the answer.

During Prohibition, an outlaw subculture grew up and prospered in order to serve the palates and tastes of Americans who came to regard the privilege of drinking as an inalienable right. With the end of Prohibition, however, the mass of that outlaw subculture was once again assimilated into the mainstream of acceptable society, and only a small percentage of the members of that subculture diverted their talents into still other illegal adventures. There is no real reason to suspect that the same will not be true with the decriminalization of the remaining categories of victimless crime.

If the prostitute and her pimp can establish themselves as recognized entrepreneurs in a legitimate endeavor, there is no particular need to mug the patrons. On the contrary, the concept of business good will is an incentive for insuring that the girl is healthy and that the patron's physical security is assured. If the smut peddlers are assured the right to ply their wares in a corner of town, without the threat of police harassment, the inducement to sell only to consenting adults is very real. If drug users have an open market where they can buy quality drugs at reasonable prices, the risk of imprisonment where drug access is limited becomes a real threat and robberies for drug money ought to diminish. Abuses will still remain just as current liquor regulations are violated. Dealing with such abuses will remain the problem of governmental regulatory agencies. Removing such matters from the mainstream of criminal prosecution, however, will result in a far safer society.

Time and time again, students of the criminal-law process point out the numbers of police man-hours spent in investigating and prosecuting victimless crimes. In order to make the point more vivid, however, an illustration of the process is helpful. Take the case of a routine prostitution arrest. First, the policeman must find a woman who apparently is selling sexual favors. After a certain amount of experience, a policeman can spot a prostitute, but no law-enforcement officer is infallible. They make mistakes, and no one can correctly estimate how many women sitting innocuously at bars or standing innocently on street corners have been annoyed or even terrified by strange men who approach them and indicate a certain predisposition to pay for sex. After a real prostitute is found, and the contract entered, the officer proceeds to make the arrest. Now the paperwork begins. A criminal complaint is typed and filed with the judge who conducts the preliminary arraignment and preliminary hearing. The officer must also prepare a report for the police file. Generally, the arresting officer checks for prior arrests and convictions, and utilizes whatever personnel is required to make this check. The arresting officer, along with a prosecuting attorney, then appears at the preliminary hearing. If all goes smoothly, the defendant appears voluntarily. If not, court personnel must attempt to locate the prostitute and bring her before the bar of justice. At the preliminary hearing, at least three public servants paid by the taxpayer will be present: the arresting officer, the prosecuting attorney, and the judge. In all likelihood, more public servants will be present: the judge's secretary or stenographer, a public defender for the indigent defendant, and perhaps a deputy sheriff to haul the prostitute back to jail if a *prima facie* case is found and bail increased. After the hearing, another piece of paper is typed and filed: the judge's disposition of the case. If the matter is bound over to court, the file is then forwarded to the clerk of court's office and the district attorney's office for further processing. At the clerk of court's office, the case is docketed by a secretary, and arrangements made for preparing still another piece of paper: an information or indictment depending upon the particular jurisdiction involved. If the grand-jury system is used, an indictment is prepared and the matter referred to a grand jury that consists of anywhere from one to several dozen persons. The arresting officer must once again testify and relate to the grand jury the facts as he recalls them. The grand jury then acts on the indictment and sends it to the court. After indictment, the matter is set down for arraignment at which time the prostitute is formally advised of the charges against her. She then enters her plea. At the arraignment, there will be the judge, his stenographer, the prosecuting attorney, a deputy sheriff, and probably a public defender. If a plea of not guilty is entered or if the defendant stands mute, a date is set for trial. Depending upon defense counsel, pretrial motions might very well have been entered requiring still another court appearance by the arresting officer, along with the prosecuting attorney, the trial judge, and his stenographer. If the issues presented by the pretrial motions are troublesome, the court may require the district attorney's office to file a memorandum of law, which consumes several more hours or even days. The court may also have its law clerk, paid by the taxpayers, do legal research on the case. If the pretrial motions are denied, a typed document denying the motions is filed with the clerk of courts and the matter is set down for trial. Trial dates are seldom met, and the arresting officer may spend anywhere from one day to several weeks pacing the halls and corridors of the courthouse waiting for the case to come to trial. At last, the case comes to trial and the matter is tried before a judge, his stenographer, a prosecuting attorney, the arresting officer, and a jury of twelve citizens. There is no such thing as a short jury trial, and the matter will at least consume a half a day for all the public servants involved. After a verdict of guilty is entered, sentence is imposed that can range from a fine without probation to imprisonment. All of this— literally hundreds of man-hours from dozens of people—

to convict one prostitute. Is it any wonder that a frustrated Philadelphia judge complained about chipmunks while wolves roamed the streets free?

Like all in life, human resources are limited. There is only so much that the criminal-law process can accomplish. When its efforts are diluted by treating as criminal human behavior that only offends another person's sensibilities and not another person's life, liberty, or property, then the effectiveness of the entire system is jeopardized. By taking cops off the street and putting them in courthouses waiting to testify against prostitutes, a human resource is underemployed. By deluging prosecutors, judges, and juries with cases involving victimless crimes, attention and effort are sidetracked from the primary purpose of criminal prosecution: promoting domestic tranquillity by convicting persons who threaten life, liberty, or property. There must be a reordering of priorities within the criminal-law system if it is to be made effective. Obnoxious behavior ought not to be the test for criminality, and crimes should be construed to mean only actions that jeopardize life, liberty, or property. The social problems associated with prostitution, "deviate" sexual behavior, pornography, drug possession and trafficking, gambling, and public drunkenness cannot be resolved by the criminal law process. Other remedies must be sought for such social evils. Criminal law ought to be confined to criminal behavior that involves real and immediate victims who suffer risk of life, liberty, or property because of another's actions. Until this realization is made, the criminal-law process will continue beleaguered under the weight of the task society has cast on its shoulders. Policemen and our courts are not equipped to deal with chipmunks. The chipmunks must be released from the jaws of criminal justice so that the wolves can be captured and punished.

Eight:

Abortion—
The Victims the Law
Cannot Protect *

In *Roe* v. *Wade* 410 U.S. 113, 93 S.Ct. 705, 35
L.Ed. 2d 147 (1973) and *Doe* v. *Bolton* 410 U.S. 179, 93
S.Ct. 739, 35 L.Ed. 2d 147 (1973), the United States Supreme Court invalidated a century-long tradition of allowing the states to protect fetal life through statutes
that punished under the sanctions of criminal law the willful and intentional termination of pregnancy. The pro-
abortionists' argument often paralleled the premises used
by the opponents of victimless crime. Essentially, they
postulated that no one has the right to interfere with the
manner in which a woman decides to use her body or any
resultant life therein. Nothing could be further from the
truth. There is an obvious "victim" of an abortion: the
fetus. The very purpose of the abortion is to extinguish
fetal life and thereby eliminate the meddlesome intrusion
that embryonic human life happens to cause the individual

*The author's views on abortion as presented here parallel his original
comments as they appeared in *U.S. Catholic,* Chicago, Illinois (September,
1973) and *America,* America Press, New York, New York (August 10,
1974). The author is grateful to both *U.S. Catholic* and *America* for
initially giving him the forum to present his opinions therein.

woman bearing such life. It is certainly arguable that the fetus, as merely the embryo of human life, does not deserve the full protection of the law. More philosophically, the question can be framed in terms of the transition point at which an embryo becomes human for purposes of human personage within meaning of the law. That moment may be at birth, at conception, or, as the Supreme Court held, at the third trimester of pregnancy. Regardless of the point at which the fetus is considered human, however, the fetus is clearly the victim of an abortion, and an examination of the majority opinions in the Roe and Doe cases on abortion tends to indicate that the Supreme Court agrees.

In both *Roe* and *Doe,* the majority opinions by Justice Blackmun start from the premise that women have *no* constitutional right to abortions. The narrower question before the court, however, was not the constitutional right of women to have abortions, but rather the inherent power of the states to prohibit women, by sanction of *criminal* law, from procuring abortions. In opposition to such state regulatory power, the Supreme Court held that a woman's constitutional right of *privacy* precluded the state from preventing her by threat of criminal punishment from receiving an abortion on demand during the first trimester of pregnancy. In the second trimester, the court held that the state could regulate abortion, not for its historic purpose of preserving fetal life, but rather only for the intention of promoting the mother's health. Only in the last trimester of pregnancy did the court preserve the possibility of criminally proscribing abortions by statute in order to preserve the life of the child by threat of imprisonment.

This new formula for allowing abortion during the first six months of pregnancy while punishing it when procured in the last three months was criticized by many religious groups, including members of the Catholic clergy and laity. Terrence Cardinal Cooke, Archbishop of New York, labeled the Supreme Court's action as "shocking." John Cardinal Dearden, Archbishop of Detroit, denounced the decision in a time of "heightened concern for the sacredness and value of human life and dignity" as a tragic step backward from a commitment to the sanctity of all human life. John Cardinal Krol, president of the National Council of Catholic Bishops, deplored the decision as "an unspeakable tragedy." The Society for a Christian Commonwealth attacked Justice William Brennan, the only Catholic on the Court, who voted with the majority, and called for his formal excommunication from the Catholic Church. Such a response by an articulate and intelligent segment of the American populace indicates a basic unawareness about the realities and limits of criminal law because, in the final analysis, fetal lives are the victims the criminal-law system cannot protect.

Persons arguing for the constitutional validity of criminal statutes punishing abortions demonstrate basic ignorance of the realities of criminal law. Criminal law only begins to function when there is a complainant. In the instance of crime with victims, the victim goes to the police and reports the incident for investigation and prosecution. In cases of victimless crimes, special undercover police units are established to seek out prostitutes, gamblers, drug users, and other similar offenders in order to obtain evidence against them. Abortion, however, fits into neither of these detection procedures.

The aborted fetus is hardly in a position to initiate a complaint and subsequent police investigation and prosecution against the would-be mother. Undercover police tactics in this area are also extraordinarily ineffective. Policemen cannot start approaching pregnant women, asking them if they want an abortion, and then arrest them when they answer affirmatively. That tactic might be adaptable to fit the crime of prostitution or gambling, but even there, undercover policemen must be careful to walk the line between advertising availability and entrapment. The circumstances surrounding the abortion and the decision to abort belie the effectiveness of the usual procedures necessary to initiate criminal prosecution.

In a criminal prosecution, it is axiomatic that the prosecution must offer evidence of the *corpus delecti* by proving all the elements of the offense—literally, production of the body of the deceased through the sworn testimony of a person who saw the corpse and can identify the cause of death. Even in the case of infanticide, the murder yields a dead body that must be concealed if the crime is to go undetected. In the case of abortion, however, there is no recognizable human body.

At the end of a month, the fetus is less than a fourth inch in length. Its heart is pulsating and pumping blood, and backbone and spinal canal are only beginning to form. It has no eyes, nose, or ears. The digestive system is just beginning to form. Only small buds that will eventually become arms and legs are visible.

At the end of the second month, the fetus is approximately one and one-eighth inches long and weighs about one-thirtieth of an ounce. A face with features is beginning to form, but eyelids are definitely fused together. The arms and legs are just beginning to show divisions into arms, elbows, forearm, and head, thigh, knee, lower leg, and foot. The taillike end of the fetus, visible at one month, is just beginning to disappear.

At the end of the first trimester, the fetus is about three inches long and weighs approximately one ounce. Arms, hands, fingers, and legs, feet, and toes are fully formed though still miniature in appearance. Nails begin to appear on fingers and toes. The ears are just beginning to take shape. The eyes are already developed, but the eyelids are still fused together. A heartbeat can now be easily detected.

At the end of the fourth month, the fetus is about seven inches and weighs nearly four ounces. The heartbeat is strong, and the skin is a bright pink and transparent covered with a fine downlike hair. The skeletal formation is now distinctive throughout the body, but the head is disproportionately larger than the body. The eyes, ears, nose, and mouth are beginning to resemble human form, and eyebrows appear on the face. It is only at the end of the fifth month that the fetus begins to take on an appearance that is typically human.

Given the uncharacteristic human form of the fetus, and its relative smallness, the woman who undergoes an abortion or the person who administers it can easily dispose of the body. Furthermore, the essential intimacy of the fetus-mother relationship makes the knowledge of the pregnancy, and concomitant discovery of abortion, an utter impracticality. It was only in the cases of bungled abortions where the women sought revenge on the persons who administered them that the possibility of prosecution ever came into being.

Once a woman becomes obviously pregnant or gives birth to her child, the secrecy of the mother-fetus relationship is destroyed and societal awareness of the child's existence can operate to protect, promote, and foster fetal life. In *Roe* v. *Wade, supra,* and *Doe* v. *Bolton, supra,* the United States Supreme Court recognized this possibility and allowed criminal prosecution of abortions performed during the third trimester of pregnancy. Even a child born into the most primitive tribal community cannot disappear without someone noting the absence. A woman more than six-months pregnant is usually not able to become unpregnant without her peers noting the change. For these reasons, infanticide or abortion at an advanced stage of pregnancy can be dealt with by criminal law. Before that, however, criminal law cannot protect the hidden victims of abortion.

It is also necessary to understand the perspective of the woman who decides to abort. Childbearing is generally an emotional experience. It may bring great joy or serious depression, but hardly ever nonchalance. For the woman who is tormented by the reality of her pregnancy and the prospect of childbirth, the strictures of criminal law are not relevant. After all, a criminal statute only prosecutes a *fait accompli*, and the prospect of ultimate apprehension and punishment is not a relevant determinant for a woman who is tortured by her pregnancy and opts for an abortion. Once the psychological commitment to abort your own fetus is made, the problem is *how* to achieve the end, not the abstract punishment that the criminal law provides. Such emotionalism, coupled with the knowledge that the chances of police awareness or investigation are nebulous, precludes any deterrent effect whatsoever of criminal-abortion statutes. It is estimated that in the year preceding the *Roe* and *Doe* cases, there were one million abortions in America. In the first year after the decision, the estimated number of legal abortions was again placed at one million.

In reaching its results in the *Roe* and *Doe* cases, it is logical to assume that the Justices of the Supreme Court were aware of the present difficulties in enforcing abortion statutes. As Oliver Wendell Holmes often fondly observed, the fact that men are appointed to the Supreme Court does not mean that they no longer read their daily newspapers. In simple terms, the court's decisions were merely a legal justification for reaching the result that women should not be thrown in jail for terminating their pregnancies. In so doing, however, the court did not give women the carte-blanche authority to procure abortions during the first six months of pregnancy. By affirmatively withholding an explicit constitutional right to abortions, the court was inviting state legislatures to pursue alternative regulation of abortions. In other words, the Supreme Court was implicitly advising that, even though the usage of criminal law was not appropriate for protecting fetal life, perhaps the usage of civil law would not be constitutionally objectionable.

An obvious response to this invitation to use the power of civil law to protect fetal life has been the passage of freedom-of-conscience statutes, which provide that doctors, nurses, and private hospitals have the right to free exercise of religion that encompasses the right to say "No" when asked to participate in another's willful termination of pregnancy. Such a civil-law statute does not use the threatening and formidable language of former criminal statutes that promised to punish those who received or administered abortions. Though less stringent in tone, however, freedom-of-conscience statutes are effective in obviating complicity by unwilling medical personnel in another's decision to abort. Furthermore, by statutorily creating a climate that allows religious freedom of conscience, the morality of eliminating fetal life can be openly discussed and debated without the threat of criminal punishment, thereby fostering an atmosphere where fetal life is protected not by force of law but rather by the power of moral persuasion.

Another situation where civil law can be effective in protecting fetal life where the sanctions of criminal law proved illusory is in preventing women from being forced by husbands or other third parties to undergo unwanted abortions. To prevent such an abuse of another's freedom of conscience, civil statutes can be enacted that provide that all abortions can only be performed upon the certification of the patient's family physician and an examining psychiatrist that such an abortion will not be to the detriment of the psychological health of the woman. As a practical matter, such certification will be easily obtained by the woman who *wants* an abortion. Yet, in the instance of the woman who is being pressured into procuring an abortion that she does not desire, there would be a medical safety valve that a doctor could use on behalf of the patient whose true will was too timid to be asserted.

Other areas of civil law must be explored to answer legal vacuums created by eliminating criminal punishment for abortion and abortionists. The rights of the father-husband during the wife's pregnancy must be examined. The continuing obligations of parents toward their unmarried pregnant daughter remain fraught with difficulties. What about the juvenile who wants an abortion when her parents object? What about the juvenile who wants her child but is forced to undergo an abortion? Such legal questions are presently unanswered, and can only be addressed by the courts after state legislatures define such rights by statutes. Until then, it is well to recognize that such matters involve the usage of civil, not criminal, law.

Criminal statutes outlawing abortion have always been empty words without substance in the real world. They have been far removed from the realities that accompany the decision to abort. Fetuses are, and have always been, the victims of abortion. Whether the statutes made it legal, illegal, or extralegal, fetuses have always been the victims that criminal law cannot protect. Some things have always remained outside the scope of law and more properly are left to the sound moral discretion of the people involved. Such is abortion. One million illegal abortions per annum before the Supreme Court's decision in *Roe* and *Doe*. One million legal abortions per annum after the decisions. In short, nothing had really changed except that an unenforceable criminal statute had been deleted from the annals of criminal law.

Nine:

Plea Bargaining— The Prosecutor, Not the Jury, Decides

Arlen Specter was a bright, young, ambitious attorney who had already made an impact on history. He had authored the controversial "single-bullet" theory of the Jack Kennedy assassination, which explained how so many wounds could have been caused by the lone assassin while firing so relatively few shots. Specter then went on to become a Republican district attorney in the predominately Democratic city of Philadelphia. In November of 1973, however, while harboring not-so-secret ambitions to run in the 1974 Pennsylvania gubernatorial election, Arlen Specter was to meet an unexpected Waterloo. In running for re-election as Philadelphia's district attorney, Specter was upset by a political unknown, Emmet Fitzpatrick. The issue on which Fitzpatrick was able to capitalize in order to upset the glib and glamorous Specter was basic: plea bargaining. Surprisingly, Emmet Fitzpatrick did not accuse Specter of abusing the powers of his office by being too lenient on criminals and bargaining away their convictions. Instead, Fitzpatrick complained that District Attorney Specter refused to plea bargain and instead caused a considerable court backlog by taking a hard line in prosecution. Fitzpatrick promised that, if elected, he would use plea bargaining more vigorously and more frequently than Specter had.

After his election, District Attorney Fitzpatrick, true to his word, instituted a widespread policy of plea bargaining. Basically, plea bargaining is negotiating a quick and simple resolution of criminal charges by convincing the defendant to plead guilty to some charges (usually lesser charges) in exchange for which the prosecution drops other charges (usually the most serious charges). The agreement can take a variety of forms and may include the provision that the prosecution recommends a specified sentence to the court, and if the court does not impose that sentence, the defendant reserves the right to withdraw the guilty plea.

One of District Attorney Fitzpatrick's first experiences in plea bargaining is illustrative of the process. The defendant had been charged with first-degree murder, which carries a mandatory sentence of life imprisonment in Pennsylvania. The new Philadelphia District Attorney had agreed to accept a plea of guilty to murder in the second degree instead of pursuing the premeditated-murder conviction. Second-degree murder carried only a maximum punishment of ten to twenty years imprisonment. The bargain was struck between the prosecution and the defense, and the plea was to be entered before the court. After hearing the facts of the case that accompanied a guilty plea colloquy, the judge refused to accept the plea because the facts clearly and unequivocally supported a conviction for first-degree murder.

The District Attorney's Office was adamant. Since there is more than one judge in Philadelphia, the solution was simple: enter the same plea before a different judge. Unfortunately, however, the second judge agreed with the first and he would not be a party to accepting a plea to second-degree murder where the facts clearly indicate murder in the first degree. A third judge was tried with the same result. The defendant was guilty by his own admission to first-degree murder, and the first-degree murder conviction should not be bargained away for the sake of judicial economy. Finally, after selecting a fourth judge, Fitzpatrick's office was able to secure a judge who would accept the guilty plea to the reduced charge.

The story of Fitzpatrick's difficulty in implementing his policy of plea bargaining to reduce judicial backlog points to the basic deficiency with plea bargaining: there is no necessary correlation between the plea and the actuality of the crime committed by the defendant. The very concept of plea bargaining involves giving the defendant a break in exchange for his plea of guilty. On the other hand, plea bargaining can be used to effect the exact opposite, namely to fit the charge with the actual offense committed by the defendant.

In Allentown, Pennsylvania, an elderly man who had a history of arrests for public drunkenness was charged with burglary and arson. The police investigation revealed that the defendant, apparently in a drunken stupor, crawled through the cellar window of an old convent building in order to sleep it off. Upon awakening, and still not in complete control of his faculties, the old man attempted to leave but found to his dismay that the only exit was locked. Not remembering his means of access, the defendant decided that the only way out was through the door, and he was bound and determined to get through that locked door. In his deteriorated mental state, the defendant decided to burn the door down, so he jammed paper all around the door frame and set it aflame. Fortunately, the smoke from the fire was quickly spotted and firemen arrived at the scene promptly to extricate the defendant and to save the building from being engulfed in flames.

Under Pennsylvania law, burglary is the unauthorized entrance into a building for the purpose of committing a crime. The drunken man's entrance into the building was unauthorized and he did commit the crime of arson while inside. A very technical reading of the burglary statute would prohibit such conduct. During the course of a plea bargain, both the prosecution and the defense agreed that the defendant's conduct hardly fell into any objective reading of the intent of the burglary statute. Consequently, a plea was entered and accepted by the court to the third-degree felony of risking a catastrophe. The real offense committed by the defendant was that he risked the lives of the several nuns who lived upstairs in the old convent building as well as his own. It was appropriate that he ought to be convicted of that crime. Through adroit use of the plea-bargaining process by both prosecution and the defense, the charge was made to fit the actualities of the crime.

The contrast between the Philadelphia plea bargain where the defendant's plea did not actually reflect his crime and the Allentown plea where the agreement to the reduced charge was more appropriate than the crime charged indicates the dilemma posed by plea bargaining. Plea bargaining is one of the lawyer's most innovative and imaginative accommodations with the realities of criminal law. Courts have become backlogged with the sheer volume of cases being funneled into the system. Yet the political realities of life are that legislators are not prepared to add to the public payrolls the number of judges, prosecutors, and auxiliary personnel to handle the increased caseload.

Plea bargaining did not arise because prosecutors and

defense lawyers do *not* want to try cases. On the contrary, lawyers who are attracted to that type of work enjoy the glamour and excitement of the trial situation. From the trial lawyer's perspective, there is nothing as dull as standing in front of a judge and entering a guilty plea. It is routine, repetitious, and boring. It requires no imagination and little skill to handle a guilty plea. In an attempt, however, to cope with the sheer volume of work to be done with too few prosecutors and judges to do it, plea bargaining has supplanted to a large extent the trial of cases. Offer the defendant a deal that is better from his viewpoint than risking conviction on a more serious offense. That is how plea bargaining arose until it became a respected prosecutorial tool in handling court backlog. Yet it involves a basic alteration of our constitutional form of government in that the prosecutor, not the jury, decides the ultimate issue of guilt or innocence. In other words, by virtue of plea bargaining, the prosecutor determines as a practical matter that the defendant is not guilty of certain offenses but guilty of others.

Presently there is a new trend growing among prosecutors to limit their own authority in plea bargaining. The impetus for this development came from a 1973 report by the National Advisory Commission on Criminal Justice Standards and Goals, which argued that plea bargaining should ultimately be phased out completely. While not in total harmony with the idea of the elimination of plea bargaining, many prosecutors have begun taking a hard line on crimes of violence, notably murders, rapes, and robberies, and have adopted an all-or-nothing attitude toward the handling of such crimes. Either the defendant pleads guilty to the crime as charged, or the case goes to the jury for its determination of guilt or innocence.

This selective prosecution of certain specified crimes of violence is an admirable effort at restoring the actualities of criminal law to its theoretical framework. Yet the fact that it is selective reveals an inarticulated assumption on the part of such prosecutors. There are simply too many types of activities that are labeled crimes yet do not belong in the criminal justice forum cluttering up our courtrooms. Under our system of government, implementation and administration of criminal law is for the prosecutors, but deciding what conduct ought to be criminal is exclusively a matter for the legislature. Because state legislators are not fulfilling their constitutional obligations in passing only reasonable legislation and repealing old and foolish laws, prosecutors have been forced to decide which laws are important and which laws can be bargained away. Unfortunately, selective enforcement of criminal statutes without plea bargaining is as much a perversion of our constitutional system of government as is plea bargaining. Until legislators enact new criminal codes that specify criminal behavior with requisite specificity and eliminate as criminal human conduct that merely offends the sensibilities of others without offending another's life or property, such accommodations by prosecutors with the realities of life will remain inevitable. Plea bargaining has arisen and flourished because of legislative lethargy, not because of prosecutorial misconduct.

Assuming that realistic criminal codes are adopted and assuming that legislators are willing to adequately staff the criminal-law process with the judges, prosecutors, and auxiliary personnel needed to try cases, plea bargaining ought to be limited by statute. Plea bargaining by the defense ought to be an option only for the first and second offenses or only where the defendant indicates that he will supply the prosecutors with evidence and testimony in other prosecutions. Absent such conditions, all offenders ought to either plead guilty to the crime as charged or face a jury of their peers to determine guilt or innocence. In our system of government, the jury is the finder of facts and that role ought not to be transferred to the prosecutor. In instances of first or second offenders, or in circumstances where the defendant cooperates in bringing others to trial, giving such defendants "bargains" can be justified. Where an offender indicates a propensity for repeated criminal behavior and offers no tangible benefit to the administration of criminal law by testifying against his companions in crime, there is no earthly reason for bargaining away his conviction.

From the defense perspective, limiting plea bargaining by statute ought to eliminate the abuse of "overindicting" or "overcharging" defendants. One of the most frequent complaints of defendants and their lawyers is that the prosecutors multiply the crime and the charges far our of proportion to what was actually done. If plea bargaining is kept to a minimum, police and prosecutors will be more cautious in drawing up charges because it is axiomatic that the prosecution does not want to try a case that it cannot prove. Under present practice, there is no harm in overcharging because the excess charges can be used as a lever over the head of a defendant unwilling to plead guilty and further they can always be dropped. If police and prosecutors knew beforehand, however, that they could very well be stuck with the charges as originally brought, they would be more apt to scrutinize the evidence and lodge charges only for those crimes that can be proven. Within this framework, statutory guidelines restricting plea bargaining only to first and second offenses and only to circumstances where the defendant offers evidence to be used against his accomplices can go a long way toward serving the cause of substantive justice and restoring our system of justice in disputed cases to a process where the jury, not the prosecutor, decides guilt or innocence.

Ten:

Trial by Jury of the Old

It is an axiom of criminal law that, where a guilty plea is not entered, defense lawyers *always* demand a trial by jury. As in everything, there are exceptions. It is nonetheless true, however, that a trial without a jury (always an option of a criminal defendant) is regarded by counsel for the defense as nothing more than a *long* guilty plea. A judge is a professional. He is less apt to be stirred by emotion. He is aware of all the tricks of the trade. He will decide the case on the facts. He understands the rules of evidence. He will not be persuaded by defense counsel's usual rejoinder: the defense of confusion. For any time the defense can succeed in obfuscating the issues and sidelining the jury into deliberating on collateral or immaterial matters, the chances of getting a verdict favorable to the defendant are greatly enhanced. For these reasons, criminal defendants through their lawyers exercise their Sixth Amendment right to trial by jury.

Prior to the trial, the lawyers and judge reign supreme. The adjudicatory system depends wholly on the steps taken by the lawyers to bring the matter to resolution and upon the judges who presided over and ruled on the preliminary motions. Once the jury is impaneled, however, the lawyers and judge are relegated to minor functionaries in the pursuit of truth. The prosecution offers evidence of guilt. The defense rebuts the prosecution in an attempt to create a reasonable doubt. The judge tells the lawyers and the jury what the applicable law is. But the jury decides the facts and therein rests ultimate power. The jury decides who should be believed, who should be doubted. It can accept the prosecution's testimony and still find insufficient evidence to support a hypothesis of guilt. It is the jury, after all, that announces "guilty" or "not guilty." In this regard, it is worthy of note that juries do not find people "innocent." It is a misnomer of the popular press that juries return verdicts of "innocent." The factual determination of the jury is limited solely to a legal conclusion. The jury either believes the prosecution established evidence of guilt beyond a reasonable doubt or holds that the prosecution's evidence did not convince them to the requisite degree of moral certitude. The defendant is, therefore, not guilty beyond a reasonable doubt. There is no requirement that the jury's verdict actually conform to the facts of the case. If the jury errs and releases a criminal, no further action can be taken to correct the blunder. It is the jury's factual determination that controls, and the assumption that truth and justice are thereby served is implicit in the dialectic process of clashing opponents in the courtroom. The supposition, however, is unsupported by empirical data, but so long as absolute truth is incompatible with the human condition, the jury system shall endure as a monument to a serious, rational, noble effort to convict the guilty and protect the innocent. To understand its operation, the details of jury selection must be examined.

On March 23, 1974, Ernie Burton was sitting in Allentown, Pennsylvania, in a bar called the "Caboose" with a twenty-year-old woman who had twice in her young life been convicted of prostitution. In Pennsylvania, the legal age for drinking is twenty-one, so the woman should never have been there. Unfortunately, she was, along with seventeen other persons, sixteen men and one other woman. The twenty-year-old woman and Ernie Burton got into an unspecified dispute that day, and Burton knocked her off the bar stool and began kicking her. He was promptly hauled out of the Caboose that Saturday afternoon at 3:00 P.M. and it appeared that the ruckus was over. Approximately two hours later, a visitor to the Allentown area entered the bar in search of a public telephone. It would be the last telephone call he would ever make. Ernie Burton returned to the Caboose at the same time, emptied five gallons of gasoline on the floor near the entrance, and ignited the flowing gasoline. When the match struck, the gasoline exploded, and the patrons at the Caboose scrambled for the rear exit. They found to their dismay that the rear door was nailed shut to keep out burglars. It also sealed in the patrons at the Caboose and, of the eighteen inside that day, nine died and the other nine suffered severe injuries, including in some cases the loss of fingers. With that single act, Ernie Burton joined the ranks of the nation's mass-murderers.

Ernie Burton was not a very clever felon. There was at least one eyewitness to the crime. Burton also confessed to the police that he had set the fire. As the trial date approached, however, it was clear that Ernie Burton was going to exercise his Sixth Amendment right to trial by jury. His able defense lawyers argued an esoteric point of Pennsylvania law that a confession is inadmissible where the defendant was not aware of the nature of the crime to which he was confessing. In Burton's case, Public Defenders Fred Lanshe and Tom Troudt argued that

Burton confessed to arson, not murder. Because he was unaware that people had actually died in the fire, their logic concluded that his voluntary confession should not be used against him. There was still the problem of the eyewitness to the crime, but one step at a time, and on to jury selection.

The Burton case presented classic problems in jury selection. Ernie Burton was black, hence the expected maneuvering to secure a racially unbiased jury in predominately white Lehigh County. The Caboose fire also received substantial media attention, nationally, internationally, and, of course, locally. The jury is required by the Constitution to be free of any bias from such adverse pretrial publicity and this problem also had to be surmounted. Furthermore, the magnitude of the crime itself might prejudice the jurors. Nine homicides. Nine aggravated assaults that included the most severe of injuries. Arson. A series of other related charges, including causing or risking a catastrophe and recklessly endangering human life. In the face of these monumental problems, jury selection began.

The process of examining potential jurors is called *voir dire*, literally, to speak the truth. It involves a preliminary examination under oath of all prospective jurors to insure that each juror shall be fair and unbiased. In the Burton case, sixty-nine potential jurors were examined before a jury of twelve and two alternates was finally selected. Each juror was examined by the court, the prosecution, and defense outside the hearing of other prospective jurors. A name was selected at random from the 100-odd members of the jury panel previously assembled. That one person then went to the courtroom where the case of *Commonwealth* v. *Burton* would be tried and the prospective juror was initially examined by the trial judge. The judge asked preliminary questions that are routinely asked in *voir dire*. If the commonwealth would prove its case beyond a reasonable doubt, would you return a verdict of guilty? If the commonwealth failed to prove its case as required by law, would you acquit the defendant? Do you personally know any of the participants in the trial, including the defendant, the lawyers on both sides, or the witnesses scheduled to testify? Would the fact that the defendant is black affect you in your deliberation on defendant's guilt or innocence? Have you read anything in the newspaper that causes you to have a fixed opinion concerning defendant's guilt or innocence? Can you approach this matter with a clear and open mind starting from the premise that the law presumes the defendant innocent? Would the fact that you would be sequestered during the trial of this matter, for weeks and possibly months, cause you to be angry with the defendant? Such were the preliminary questions asked by the court in the first instance.

After the court concluded its initial examination, then both sides, prosecution and defense, were given an opportunity to explore, in depth, the areas touched on by the judge, and to examine other facets of the juror's personality. Where one female indicated strong religious convictions, District Attorney George J. Joseph spoke at great length with her concerning her conception of God's law versus man's law, and where her obligation stood. When she replied, "Render to Caesar the things that are Caesar's and to God the things that are God's," District Attorney Joseph was satisfied that the woman could fulfill her sacred oath as a juror and return a verdict of guilty if the commonwealth proved its case. In commenting on that particular episode later, a local reporter wrote that it was a moment of "gentle beauty" with the lawyers and court running a classroom in democracy where the ideals of our Founding Fathers were dramatized in the flesh.

Not all incidents during the *voir dire* in the Burton

murder trial were scenes of gentle beauty. At one point, Ernie Burton got into a violent verbal clash with his lawyers because they wanted to dismiss an elderly gentleman from service because the man obviously had a serious hearing problem. When the defendant's wishes prevailed over the judgment of his lawyers, the district attorney exercised his right to remove the juror, who proved unsatisfactory to him. After all, a juror must be able to hear the evidence.

Another episode less verbal and more physical involved Ernie Burton's refusal to remain in the courtroom. As proved to be his custom throughout the proceedings, Ernie Burton got up from the defense table and waved "so long" to everyone, indicating that he was leaving for the day. Generally, he responded to the admonitions of the court that he must remain, and with the coaxing of his lawyers, he would sit back and listen quite attentively to the proceedings. At one point, however, Burton decided that enough was enough, and when the court and his lawyer urged him to stay, he violently shoved his counsel against the counsel table. With that, several deputy sheriffs in attendance were upon him, and Burton resisted. The mace came out and was suddenly being sprayed upon Burton and anyone else in the vicinity, including his lawyers and an assistant district attorney who proved to be too close at hand. It was the only such violent outburst during the pretrial proceedings, but it demonstrated the sense of high drama that the participants felt during *voir dire.*

During the questioning of prospective jurors in *voir dire,* lawyers for both sides were searching for personality clues that might indicate latent sympathies for either the prosecution or the defense. If a juror is asked whether or not he would, for personal reasons, be reluctant to return a verdict of "guilty" even if the charges were proved beyond a reasonable doubt, and if he replies emphatically, "Absolutely not," the prosecution may greet his determinedness with delight, but the defense will surely frown upon such single-mindedness.

In the process of reviewing prospective jurors, both the prosecution and defense can attempt to disqualify the potential trier of facts by convincing the court that the answers indicate that the juror is prejudiced against the defendant or has already predetermined guilt or innocence. For example, in Ernie Burton's case, a woman was dismissed "for cause" when she indicated that she was prejudiced against blacks. Many others were similarly dismissed when they indicated that they had a fixed opinion of guilt based upon newspaper stories that they had previously read.

In addition to challenges "for cause," each side also has a set number of "peremptory challenges," which can be used without explanation based upon hunches or personal predilections. For example, the prosecutor might be suspicious of men who wear bow ties because it indicates a certain amount of individualism and a personal inclination not to go along with the group. Of course, no trial judge could properly dismiss a prospective juror because he wears a bow tie, so the prosecution, without explanation, merely exercises a peremptory challenge. In the Burton case, both sides had twenty peremptory challenges, with the defense actually using about five times as many as the district attorney. Even the defense, however, did not use all its peremptory challenges thereby indicating to the court that it was satisfied with the composition of the jury.

Many lawyers believe that the process of selecting the jury is the single most crucial factor in determining the result of the trial, and there are occasions where substantial amounts of money are spent on in-depth compilations of psychological profiles of each potential juror. There were reports that, in the Mitchell-Stans trial in federal court in New York on charges stemming from the Vesco affair, the defense spent over $100,000 in obtaining psychological profiles of all prospective jurors. When the process of *voir dire* began, counsel for the defense used this information to obtain a jury composed of white, working-class, high-school-educated subscribers to the *New York Daily News,* and systematically excluded, through adroit use of peremptory challenges, all college-educated, white-collar workers who read the *New York Times.* The defense assumption, ostensibly correct, was that such a jury would be more susceptible to accept their version of the facts than a better-educated, more-informed jury. The verdict returned in the Mitchell-Stans case was, of course, "not guilty," but one can only speculate as to the verdict of other jurors dismissed during *voir dire* if they had heard the same evidence.

After the jury panel was sworn and ready to proceed in the case of *Commonwealth* v. *Ernie Burton,* the jury was seated, the witnesses brought into the courtroom, and District Attorney George Joseph was set to begin his opening statement. Seated directly behind Ernie Burton was the eyewitness to the crime. Apparently Burton had hoped that the witness would not come to court to testify for the eyewitness was also black, and in the vernacular, a "brother," but so also were sixteen of the victims of the Caboose fire. The witness was prominently there, and the trial was ready to start. The question of the usage of Burton's prior confession remained in doubt, but with the eyewitness, the question became academic. After six grueling days of jury selection involving an in-depth examination of sixty-nine jurors, Ernie Burton decided to plead guilty, and the service of the twelve jurors was no longer necessary. The guilty plea was entered, and Ernie Burton was sentenced to life imprisonment.

In the Burton case, the process of jury selection was more than a lesson in democracy. It involved psychological warfare where the district attorney conveyed to the defendant through his poise and confidence that he was prepared to go all the way, no matter how long it took. There would be no deals, no plea bargains. Guilty to all thirty-three indictments was the only plea that was acceptable. Somewhere during the proceeding, Ernie Burton decided that no jury of reasonable men and women would ever acquit him, and he entered his plea. It was another aspect of *voir dire* that goes deeper than the mere selection of jury. As in many cases, it took the actual presence of the jury to convince the defendant that the time had come to make a realistic appraisal of his situation and to plead guilty. With that, Ernie Burton became by his own words a mass-murderer.

Voir dire is an efficient though inexpeditious means of securing a fair and unbiased jury for a defendant. Its practical limitations, however, include an inability to supply a jury of defendant's peers as contemplated by the Sixth Amendment. In the ordinary course of events, a jury panel of a set number, usually more than 100, is randomly selected from the residence rolls and impaneled for a set period of time, anywhere from a week to months. Before individuals are selected from that panel for specific cases, and prior to any legal representation of any defendant, jurors can opt out of the panel by convincing the court that an undue personal hardship would result if they were required to serve. As a practical manner, this means that anyone with any type of prior commitments in the community can secure his dismissal from jury service. In practical terms, this means the panel is composed of people with one common element: time to serve. Translated into the actualities of life, it means trial by juries of the old for it is generally older, retired people who, in effect, are willing to volunteer their time to jury service. Through the systematic exercise of opting for nonservice by younger, busier citizens, the remaining members of the panel are hardly representative of the cross section of the community as envisioned by the Founding Fathers.

One can only speculate on the effect that trials by juries of the old have on the administration of criminal justice for no empirical data can be gathered to ascertain how others who might have served would have voted on certain particular cases if they had heard the evidence. It appears, however, that the constitutional mandate of juries representing a cross section of the community can only be achieved by providing for mandatory jury service for all with only specific legislatively ordained exceptions as in the case of illness or physical inability to serve. In this manner, service would be the norm and being excused from service the exception. By enlarging the pool of persons who would be required to undergo jury service, and thereafter using the *voir dire* process to interview potential jurors, the ideals of the Sixth Amendment of trial by jury of peers, rather than trial by jury of the old, can be realized.

Eleven:

Sentencing and King Solomon

Biblical King Solomon has served as the arche-
type of judicial wisdom. Just as Solomon was able to delve
into the heart of the question of ownership of the disputed child, modern-day judges are entrusted with un-
limited discretion in the handling of the fates of convicted
felons. At the time of sentencing, judges are given a
wealth of information concerning the offender's background. Childhood history. Juvenile record. Psychological
profiles. Record of arrests and convictions. Psychiatric
evaluations. Accurate as well as inaccurate information
filters its way to the judge who is about to pronounce
sentence. From this mass of information, the judge as-
sesses the defendant's personality and character, reviews
the particular facts of the crime involved, determines the
outside parameters of punishment as set by statute, and
imposes a sentence that befits the defendant for his crime.
Such is the process of sentencing inspired by the example
of wise King Solomon. Only most judges are not Solo-
mons. On the contrary, judges tend to be provincial, prejudiced, partisan men who evaluate life from their own
backgrounds and perspectives, and flavor the sentencing

of defendants who appear before them with their own social, ethnic, and educational biases. Because of this reality, the entire sentencing procedure must be revamped.

In twentieth century American jurisprudence, the indeterminate sentence is the norm. Translated into simple terms, the indeterminate sentence means that the only substantive limitation placed on judges during sentencing is the maximum amount of punishment. For example, it is not uncommon for all punishment to be defined in terms of maximum punishment for degrees of crime:

> Felony of the first degree: No more than twenty years imprisonment
>
> Felony of the second degree: No more than ten years imprisonment
>
> Felony of the third degree: No more than seven years imprisonment
>
> Misdemeanor of the first degree: No more than five years imprisonment
>
> Misdemeanor of the second degree: No more than two years imprisonment
>
> Misdemeanor of the third degree: No more than one year imprisonment.

Within such a statutory scheme, a judge is free to sentence a person convicted of a felony of the first degree to a one- to two-year sentence while sentencing a person guilty of a misdemeanor of the first degree to a three- to five-year incarceration. More outlandishly, there are no statutory guidelines for determining whether or not a prison sentence should be dispensed with entirely by instead placing an offender on probation.

Other statutory schemes provide for a set minimum and maximum sentence within which the judge must impose punishment, e.g., felony of the first degree: no less than five and no more than twenty years of imprison-

ment. Even such systems, however, permit judges to sus-
pend sentences and allow the court the option of placing
the convicted defendant on probation. As is obvious to
even a casual observer of America's criminal-justice system, there is a world of difference between being sentenced to prison and being placed on probation.

The other biggest factor in determining actual service
of time in prison is the usage of concurrent or consecutive
sentences where the offender is found guilty of multiple
crimes or has already been incarcerated on other charges.
For example, assume that a rapist kidnaps his victim,
beats her, sexually assaults her, and then uses her to perform unnatural sexual acts. In most jurisdictions, the perpetrator of such a crime would be guilty of kidnapping,
rape, sodomy, and assault, four separate and distinct offenses each with its own prescribed punishment. Assume
that the defendant is thereafter sentenced to ten to twenty
years on the kidnapping, five to ten on the rape, three
to five on the sodomy, and one to two on the assault. The
only real question to the defendant is how much jail time
before he is eligible for parole. In order to answer this
question, it must be decided whether or not the sentences
are to run concurrently or consecutively. If the sentences
are to run concurrently, it means that all sentences are
to run at that same time or covering the same time period.
In other words, the only significant sentence is the largest
one for purposes of computing jail time because all other
sentences are being served while the kidnapping sentence
is running. On the other hand, if the sentences are to run
consecutively, it means that one sentence must be
completed before time is served on any other sentence.
In other words, first the kidnapping sentence must be
completed before the rape sentence is served. Then, after
the rape sentence is ended, the sodomy sentence commences, and after that sentence is finished, the assault

sentence still must be satisfied. The actual jail time for consecutive sentences is, therefore, much greater than for concurrent sentences, but the general rule of law is that, unless the judge explicitly states that the sentences are to be served consecutively, all sentences run concurrently. The decision rests with the individual judge, and there is no set rule of law except judicial discretion regarding the appropriateness of using consecutive versus concurrent sentences.

Examples of differing standards applied by various judges are notorious. John A. Sinclair, a would-be revolutionary at the University of Michigan during the Vietnam War, was given nine and one-half years to ten years for possession of one marijuana cigarette until the Michigan Supreme Court reversed his conviction. See *People* v. *Sinclair*, 387 Mich. 91, 194 N.W. 2d 878 (1972). Judges have been known to sentence unemployed black males who were living with women without the benefit of marriage to three to five *years* imprisonment for possession of heroin while sentencing employed white males who were supporting their wives and children from seven to twenty-three *months* for near-fatal shootings in a barroom brawl. One of the most publicized exercises of judicial discretion and laxity is, of course, the Spiro Agnew case where the former Vice President of the United States was brought before the bar of justice by the Attorney General of his own administration and pleaded nolo contendere, i.e., I will not admit that I am guilty, but I will not contest the charges, and was thereafter given a suspended sentence and probation on charges of income-tax evasion. The law is replete with such examples, and they all stem from a common base: in twentieth century America, sentencing is exclusively within the province and discretion of the judiciary.

If the criminal-law system is going to work, determination of sentences must be taken out of the hands of the thousands and thousands of individual judges who exercise their own version of right and righteousness, and once again be premised in law. It was once a maxim of law that sentencing is properly a legislative function, and it was in the province of the legislature to decide what sentencing ought to be. Because legislators have never been particularly bright on the subject of sentencing and instead have consistently voted to demonstrate to their constituencies how vengeful they can be, the movement toward judicial discretion in sentencing inevitably grew until it fashioned itself into the chaos of today. Thousands and thousands of individual judges cannot act in concert to effect uniform substantive justice. Legislators acting in concert and establishing a system can, by statute, and by determinate sentences, go a long way toward serving justice.

The concept of indeterminate sentencing has failed. By its very definition, *indeterminate* means *indefinite*, and is, therefore, arbitrary, capricious and discriminating. It is not, however, a matter of simply returning to the days of yore where each crime had a definite punishment and no effort was made for the punishment to fit the offender. There is no reason that an eighteen-year-old youth who burglarizes a garage for the very first time in his life ought to be treated the same as the professional cat burglar who robs jewelry stores and has a history of convictions for similar offenses. The system of discretion must be premised in statute with each category being given a definite punishment.

The biggest difficulty in sentencing reform is to insure that legislatures adopt a realistic level of punishment. After all, four years in prison is an incredibly long time. If that fact escapes you, think in terms of just how many experiences your own life enjoyed in the last four years and how much your own life has changed in that time period. Furthermore, statistically, four years is more than five percent of a normal individual's lifetime, and there are not so many five percent blocks of life in anyone's life that one would voluntarily keep devoting them to jail, especially since twenty-five percent of an individual's life is already lived before he is subjected to the ordinary process of criminal law. Yet our legislators keep insisting on talking in terms of ten years, twenty years, life imprisonment, death penalty. This sensationalism of punishment only makes the use of discretionary punishment inevitable until discretion, which begins as an exception, ends up as the general rule.

Part of the blame for unrealistic levels of punishment as set by statute must also fall on the shoulders of the judiciary. Our constitution clearly and explicitly prohibits cruel punishment, but our courts have been reluctant to breathe life into this constitutional guarantee. Instead, the judiciary has invented the maxim that sentences within statutory limits are not reviewable on appeal. By refusing to decide that a twenty-year maximum for burglarizing a garage is cruel punishment, the judges have allowed alarmist legislators to control the statutory levels of punishment. The courts must fulfill their constitutional obligations to prevent cruel punishment if legislatures are ever to enact realistic standards of punishment. Once humane and realistic sentences are enacted, the goal of reform will inevitably be realized.

The next most pressing area of reform in sentencing is in correlating proper punishment with narrowly defined categories of crime. As indicated earlier, using all-encompassing classifications of crime effectively negates particularizing the elements of odious behavior that are intended to be punished. Realistic levels of punishment must be ascribed to each and every particular category of crime with each and every statutory definition of criminal behavior being spelled out in detail in order to establish a rational and graduated system of crime and punishment. Perhaps a ten-year sentence for murdering your mother-in-law during the course of a heated argument is far too long for a first offender while even the death penalty is not quite adequate for the cold-blooded assassin who kills, for hire, the President of the United States. Until such time that crime is defined with precision instead of broad, catchall categories, it will be impossible to set realistic, statutorily mandated sentences.

Under present sentencing procedures, the court is required to take into account the defendant's psychological, sociological, and psychiatric background as reflected, in part, by the defendant's arrest and conviction record. Such criteria uniformly assist the rich and the powerful at the expense of the poor, the weak, and the downtrodden. If equality under the law is to be realized, it ought not to matter in sentencing two different male first offenders for voluntary manslaughter that one is white, middle class, living with his wife and supporting his children, and employed as an aerospace engineer and that the other is black, lower class, shacking up with a woman and his two illegitimate children, and living off her welfare checks. The only relevant standard ought to be the defendant's prior record of convictions. Furthermore, instead of allowing individual trial judges to evaluate the defendant's record, the system of punishment ought to be statutorily elevated by a fixed number of years for each particular crime for each prior conviction. Such a system, of course, must necessarily distinguish between felony and misdemeanor convictions. This distinction, however, and the gradation of punishment based upon prior conviction ought to be set by law, not by individual judges.

The most pressing and crucial reform in sentencing is the exclusive use of the determinate sentence, i.e., a specified and exact time period of punishment for every crime. Instead of sentencing a convicted burglar from three to twenty years, the punishment ought to be precise. Three years for this crime for first offense. Five years for the same crime if it is the defendant's second felony conviction. Three-and-a-half years for that same crime if it is the defendant's second conviction, but the first crime was only a misdemeanor. Seven years for that same crime if it is a defendant's third or more felony conviction.

In such a system of punishment, sentencing would become a mechanical function for the judge. The judge would look to the crime, examine the offender's prior conviction record, and apply the punishment as written into law. It may be argued that such proposals are hardly in keeping with attempting to fit the punishment to the criminal, not to the crime. That may very well be so, but the American experience of expecting sentencing judges to be able to fit the punishment to the offender based upon the individual's personality, background, and arrest and conviction record is hardly commendable. A system of realistic but definite punishment for specific statutory crimes that has discretion built into the scale of punishment by providing for graduated and increasing levels of punishment for repeated offenders is the only system that can constitutionally qualify as providing for equal treatment and equal justice under the law. Our present system of discretionary punishment by diverse members of the judiciary who are unequal in talents and perceptions is arbitrary and capricious at its best. At its worst, it is susceptible to class bias, racism, and outright corruption. No one gains in such a system, not the defendants, not the lawyers who represent them, not the victims of crime, not the society and its ideal of equality under the law. The present system of sentencing must be replaced, and a whole new concept of the sentencing of convicted defendants must be examined. Realistic punishment for specific and exact crimes with discretion built into the system, and judicial discretion minimized, is an appropriate resolution in the present crisis of sentencing.

Some areas of judicial discretion in sentencing ought to be preserved, namely, the imposition of a suspended sentence, and the use of concurrent versus consecutive sentences. Even such areas of discretionary punishment, however, must be limited and subjected to law. The option of a suspended sentence ought to be statutorily restricted to situations involving a first offender who did not commit a crime of violence against a person. Concurrent sentencing, however, ought to be the statutory norm for every defendant's first two appearances before a sentencing judge. At a defendant's third appearance involving multiple crimes or incomplete previous sentences, the option of the usage of concurrent or consecutive sentences ought to be with the judges. At the fourth or subsequent appearance, however, the court ought to be required by law to impose consecutive sentences. The premise for allowing such remaining vestiges of discretionary punishment is that every first offender ought to be considered for the possibility of leniency. At the stage where a person is indicating a propensity toward a life of crime, as evidenced by a third conviction, the threat of consecutive punishment ought to be available to deter a twice-convicted offender and to allow the judiciary to safeguard society by increasing the punishment of the three-time loser. When recidivism, that is, repeated criminal activity, becomes particularly acute by virtue of a fourth offense, consecutive sentencing ought to be the mandatory punishment.

In order to allow appropriate judicial review of the areas of discretion still available to the sentencing judge in suspended sentences and concurrent versus consecutive sentencing, the right of appellate review of sentencing ought to be available to the prosecution and the defense and the trial judge ought to be required to spell out in detail the basis for his decision. Instead of allowing the basis of the exercise of limited discretion to remain locked up in the sentencing judge's head, the trial court ought to be required to list the factors that it considered in exercising the option of a suspended sentence or the option of consecutive sentencing at the time of the third encounter with the law. In this manner, limited discretion will not become unbridled, and its exercise would be reviewable on appeal.

Within the whole scheme of criminal law, the sentencing stage is the most important for purposes of effecting the objectives of the criminal-law process: (1) retribution, (2) revenge, (3) deterrence, and (4) rehabilitation. Unfortunately, however, sentencing is the most neglected area of law. There are no real statutory standards of punishment that deal with the problem of realistic punishment to fit the crime. There is no body of case law on the subject of cruel and inhuman punishment. Yet every year, countless numbers of persons are sentenced almost daily and the standards of punishment vary from state to state, from community to community, from judge to judge. If the criminal-law system is to function properly, and if justice is to be the ultimate goal, sentencing must become more than judicial capriciousness. It must be a system of realistic, rational, graduated levels of punishment intended to fit the crime and the perpetrator thereof. Until this is done, substantial reform of our criminal law will remain in its present quagmire: unevenhanded justice for the many, deterrence of the few.

Twelve:

Reversal on Appeal—
What It Means and
What It Does Not Mean

On August 11, 1962, at about 2:45 A.M., Cleveland police officers went to 2760 East 75th Street in response to a radio assignment. There they found Lester Watkins sitting at a table in the kitchen and a dead woman lying on the floor in the hallway between the kitchen and the bedroom with a partially open straight razor on her left side. Under interrogation and without the presence of counsel, Lester Watkins told the police that his wife, Frances Mullins Watkins, came at him with a razor during an argument. He retreated from this assault until he was cornered in the kitchen, and then he took out a gun and fired. As a police officer testified, Watkins orally advised him that he took the gun from his overalls and was going to scare her with it. He fired the gun and hit her, and then he called the police.

Lester Watkins was then taken by the police to the criminal-statement unit where, without the presence of counsel, he signed a written statement that was introduced as evidence at the trial by the prosecution. The written statement gave a detailed account of the events leading up to the fatal shooting. Watkins stated that he first returned home from work about 6:00 P.M. the evening of August 10, 1962. His wife was not there so he went across the street to buy some chewing tobacco. He returned home within half an hour and found his wife in bed. He asked her how she was feeling, but she replied curtly that it was none of his concern. Watkins knew his wife was angry with him because she incorrectly believed that he was having an affair with another woman. To avoid an argument, Lester Watkins returned to work in his self-employed business and did not come back home until later that evening.

Upon returning home at 10:00 P.M., Watkins fixed himself something to eat. His wife was once again absent. After finishing eating, he went to the neighborhood tavern only to find much to his dismay that his wife was already there. Wishing to avoid further argument, Watkins chose to ignore her. This further infuriated her and caused still another squabble. This time, the argument was more violent, and Frances Watkins attacked her husband, knocking him off the bar stool and slashing him on the shoulder with a straight razor.

After the confrontation, Lester Watkins remained in the bar while his wife was ushered out of the premises. Upon returning home later that evening, Watkins found that his wife had placed a chair against the door so the noise would awaken her as he entered. Still in a drunken stupor, Frances came at her husband with the straight razor. In attempting to retreat, Lester Watkins became cornered in the kitchen. Watkins then pulled from underneath his overalls a gun that he carried for his protection. He was carrying the gun because he had been robbed several times on the job. As he wrote in his statement to the police: "And I was going to shoot to frighten her, and I shot, and stood there a few minutes, and she turned around and headed toward her bedroom and fell." Watkins then called the police and told them that he was afraid of his wife because she previously cut another man to death.

At his trial for murder in the second degree, which began on January 23, 1962, Lester Watkins's testimony was substantially similar to his written statement. He testified that he carried the gun in his truck because "... I had been robbed several occasions, and beaten up, and wasn't able to work for two or three days." He continued: "Well, when I got home, I went by the truck and taken the gun out, and usually take that into the house every night." He further testified that he hid the gun from his wife under the bathtub "... because she said that she could not do much bending down." Then he told the court and the jury how his wife cornered him and how he fired the gun to scare her: "I begged her to leave me alone, and I am tired, and I worked hard all day, and will you please let me get to sleep, and she kept chasing me, and she just kept her lips in like that, and kept chasing me, and I could not go into the bathroom because there was no way out, and I could not go in the bedroom because there is no way out. She got between me and the door going to the kitchen, and I had to play like I was going in the bedroom, and she moved, and I went into the kitchen, and running like that I was afraid that the gun would fall out of my belt. I took the gun in my hand, and when I got in the kitchen I thought if I would shoot she would be getting excited and leave me alone."

Under cross-examination, Watkins testified that he never intended to shoot his wife.

Q. Where was the gun aimed when it went off, Mr. Watkins?
A. It wasn't aimed.
Q. But you did shoot the gun?
A. Yes, I did.

Q. At Frances?

A. No, sir, I wasn't pointing at her, and if I wanted to hurt her, I could have taken that chair . . . I did not point at her, and I just shot, and I was so excited.

The autopsy revealed that Frances Watkins drank twelve ounces of whisky very rapidly shortly before her death. Further evidence revealed that she was a woman of violent disposition, having been arrested some fourteen times for offenses including murder and assaults and batteries. In contrast, the evidence of Lester Watkins indicated that he was a pleasant and peace-loving man.

The prosecution offered conflicting evidence on the absence of fingerprints on the straight razor next to the decedent's body. Detective Larry March testified that he dusted the razor for prints and found none. The inference was, therefore, that Frances Watkins never had the razor in her hand, and instead it was planted there by her husband after he shot her and cleaned his prints off the razor. But Detective March's report indicated that no fingerprint search was made.

Q. And you made a statement in your report that you did not search for fingerprints. Is that correct?

A. That is right.

Q. What did you say?

A. That is right.

Other evidence produced at the trial indicated the inadequacy of the police investigation surrounding the death of Frances Mullins Watkins. Detective Jackman testified that he searched for the alleged arrest record of Frances Mullins at the Scientific Identification Unit and that he found no such record. Patrolman Joseph Mohnacky, however, produced this criminal arrest record under subpoena, and as alleged by her husband, Frances

Mullins Watkins had indeed been arrested for murder for slashing a man to death with a razor.

On January 29, 1963, the jury found Lester Watkins not guilty of murder in the second degree but guilty of manslaughter as a lesser included offense. On January 25, 1966—almost three years later—the Ohio Court of Appeals granted Lester Watkins's motion for delayed appeal. On June 11, 1969, some six-and-a-half years later, the Cleveland public defender's office was appointed counsel for Watkins after his original court-appointed counsel had died.

On appeal, the public defender's office argued on behalf of Watkins that the judgment of conviction was against the manifest weight of the evidence since the defense proved by a preponderance of the evidence that the shooting was committed in self-defense. After reviewing the facts of the case, the Ohio Court of Appeals reversed Lester Watkins's conviction as against the manifest weight of the evidence and ordered him discharged from custody. After almost seven years incarceration, Lester Watkins was free, having been found not guilty by the Ohio Court of Appeals. It was a rare act of appellate power that a prisoner should be discharged without further court action.

During the 1968 presidential elections, Richard M. Nixon campaigned throughout the country charging that the United States Supreme Court was letting convicted felons out of prison. He pledged, therefore, that, if elected, his appointees to that august body would deal more severely with criminals and that his Supreme Court would insure that, once imprisoned, convicted felons remained there.

As is often the case with political rhetoric, it did not accurately reflect reality. Appellate courts, such as the Supreme Court, are seldom in a position to order a prisoner discharged. The case of a Lester Watkins is atypical because the appellate court did not bow to the verdict of the jury. Under ordinary principles of law, appellate courts always defer to the verdict of the jury if there is any evidence whatsoever upon which the jury could reasonably rely in order to justify its result. It is only in a case where the evidence of innocence is overwhelming that an appellate court will step in and effect substantive justice by ruling that the verdict is against the manifest weight of the evidence.

Appellate forums can also release prisoners where they find that the statute under which the defendant was convicted is unconstitutional therefore, no real crime has been committed. For example, assume that the legislature of a particular state enacted a statute prohibiting persons from attending a Catholic Mass on Sunday. Assume, further, that numerous Catholics were thereafter arrested, convicted, and sentenced for their attendance at Sunday Mass. During the trial, the Catholic defendants freely admitted their participation in the alleged crime, but argued that such conduct was not criminal because the statute violated their First Amendment right to free exercise of religion. On appeal to the United States Supreme Court, the court would be totally justified in finding the statute unconstitutional and ordering the discharge of the prisoners. Again, such cases are atypical, and it is only in such limited circumstances that the United States Supreme Court would release the "criminals."

The normal business of appellate courts is to correct erroneous rulings by the trial court and remand the case for retrial. In simple terms, the appellate court tells the trial judge, "You goofed. This time do it right." As Judge Sirica was fond of observing, such directives by appellate tribunals do not mean that the higher court's judgment is morally right or intellectually sound. It simply means that, in our judicial system, the appellate courts are given the final word, and in that sense, might makes right.

Even in the landmark case of *Miranda* v. *Arizona* 384 U.S. 436, 86 S.Ct. 1602, 16 L.Ed. 2d 694 (1966), which gave indigent defendants the right to appointed counsel prior to being interrogated while in police custody, and of which Richard M. Nixon bitterly complained, there was no court order releasing the prisoner. Instead, the Supreme Court merely suppressed the confession and gave the trial court the opportunity to re-try the Miranda case before a jury using all other evidence against him except the confession. Generally, such is the nature of an appellate's court order, and therein lies the reason for the oft-used appellate expression, "Reversed and Remanded."

Even in the celebrated case of *Dr. Sam Sheppard* v. *Maxwell, Warden of Ohio Penitentiary*, 384 U.S. 333, 86 S.Ct. 1507, 16 L.Ed. 2d 600 (1966) where the Supreme Court reversed Sheppard's conviction of murdering his pregnant wife because of adverse pretrial publicity that affected the jury's deliberation, the State of Ohio was given the opportunity to re-try the prisoner. As in all cases, the decision whether or not reprosecution ought to be undertaken must be based upon a realistic assessment of the facts. Where some evidence is suppressed, the remaining evidence may or may not be sufficient to successfully prosecute. Where a confession is ruled inadmissible, other evidence available against the defendant must be evaluated. Where an inordinate length of time has already transpired, the question of witnesses' memories being clear enough to allow retrial must be addressed. A reversal of a judgment of conviction by its very nature upsets the conviction. It does not, however, automatically guarantee that the prisoner goes free. In Dr. Sam Sheppard's case, he was thereafter found not guilty at his retrial, and such is always the possibility in any second prosecution. It is erroneous to charge, however, that an appellate forum by correcting errors committed by the trial court necessarily and inevitably means letting the criminals go.

The purpose of providing for an appellate forum is to allow judges with the luxury of time and research assistants to review a prosecution. During the course of a trial, a judge is under enormous pressure to make quick, hasty and correct rulings. When a lawyer asks a question and an objection is entered, the trial judge does not have the time to recess the court and spend hours researching the applicable law. The trial judge must make an intuitive guess of the status of the law based upon his wealth of personal knowledge and experience in trying cases. It is the appellate forum that can thereafter review the court's decision, and correct it if it is in error. Such is the logic of appellate review.

In an era of judicial backlog and personal crusades by the Chief Justice of the United States for alternative mechanisms for judicial decision-making, questions inevitably arise concerning the efficiency of our appellate forums. Are appellate decisions of today the well-reasoned scholarly pieces of judicial prose that were originally contemplated by the concept of appellate review? Or are appellate decisions themselves hasty and intuitive guesses of the status of the law at a particular point in time?

Upon assuming the Chief Judgeship of the United States, the Honorable Warren Burger quickly realized that the workload entailed more than appears on the surface. Not only do Supreme Court Justices decide cases, but they also must initially determine which cases ought to be heard by the court. Through a process called *certiorari*, lawyers present to the United States Supreme Court a brief explanation of their cases, and attempt to demonstrate that the case that they are arguing is worthy of a full and detailed argument before the court. If four of the nine Justices agree, then the case is briefed and argued on its merits before the entire panel of Justices. Statistically, only a small percentage of the cases brought before the Supreme Court on *certiorari* are ultimately advanced to a final argument before the entire bench.

As Chief Burger observed, deciding which cases must be decided easily takes up as much time as actually resolving the cases brought before the court for argument on the merits. To Chief Justice Burger, the workload was onerous, and he quietly began an effort to ease his and the court's workload by authorizing a study to determine the feasibility of transferring the decisions on petitions of *certiorari* to another forum. The resultant Freund Report came back with the desired recommendations: create a mini-Supreme Court to decide what cases the Supreme Court should ultimately hear.

The Freund Report met with quick and vociferous opposition. Former Chief Justice Earl Warren publicly denounced the scheme as did Justices Brennan and Douglas. Justice Douglas even announced that the overburdening-workload argument was a myth and that the position of the Supreme Court Justice was only a four-day-a-week job. His argument is difficult to counter when it is realized that, during a given term of court, Justice Douglas was the most productive and prolific Justice writing by far the most opinions, while the Chief Justice penned the least.

The argument of the opponents of the Freund Report was that "deciding-to-decide" is probably more important in the scheme of decision-making than rendering the actual decision itself. By giving the proposed mini-Supreme Court a veto on which cases the Supreme Court actually hears, the mini-Supreme Court can effectively diminish the power of the highest court in the land. Right to court-appointed counsel for indigents. Miranda warnings. Right to counsel at line-ups. Decriminalization of abortion. It is not inconceivable that such matters could have remained outside the domain of the Supreme Court forever if they first had to pass through a mini-Supreme Court.

The problem of a backlog in the appellate forums, including the United States Supreme Court, appears not to be so much the result of volume as it does the attitude of the judiciary. Our Founding Fathers envisioned a system where the judiciary would not only be free and independent but would be composed also of dispassionate, objective men committed to truth and justice. Such are not, however, the realities of life where some men who become judges approach their task not in the search for truth but rather with the purpose of engrafting their own political ideology into the law. When ideologues are judges, no cases are routine, and every case becomes important for its potential of shattering existing precedents. *Stare decisis* was once the basic premise of the judiciary, that is, the law builds upon and evolves upon existing precedents. Such principles are no longer governing, and the judiciary has become a battleground for conservative ideologues versus liberal ideologues. Neither views the case before it with dispassion, and both attempt to use the matter before them as a vehicle for political actualization of their own preconceived conceptions of law and justice.

Within the context of judicial ideologue, the appellate forum is transformed from the place where a trial judge's errors are contested to a political arena for judicial policy-making. When each case involves momentous decisions rather than mere judicial review of the lower court, the forum creates its own backlog by changing its mission. It is only through a rededication of the judiciary to the ideals of truth, justice, and objectivity that the appellate forum can once again perform its function of correcting abuses by trial courts. Judicial ideologues, conservative or liberal, do not further that function.

Where a liberal ideologue decides a case solely within the framework of protecting the convicted felon, then the process of justice is not served and the guilty are apt to be freed. Where a conservative ideologue strains to uphold the conviction regardless of the facts of the case, then the innocent ultimately suffer. The blind matron of justice holding delicately balanced scales in her hand remains a timely model that all judges should attempt to follow. Needless to say, many judges still hold this out as their ideal. Unfortunately, however, many do not, and if the appellate process is to be understood, it must be realized what the purpose of judicial review is, and what it now has become to some of the men and women who wear judicial robes.

Thirteen:

Parole—
Life on the Installment Plan

One of the first things an observer notices about prisoners is the constant anxiety in their lives. It is a psychological torment of the worst kind. There is no certitude in their existence. The sentencing judge may very well say eight to ten years imprisonment, but there is no substance to the words. There is always the hope, embellished by jailhouse lawyers who know little to nothing about the law, that someday soon they will be free.

It merely takes the stroke of a pen to free a prisoner. A state judge filing an order on a postconviction petition or a federal judge signing a writ of habeas corpus can melt iron bars and allow a man one day a prisoner the next day to be free.

Dashed hopes where there never should have been hope are common in prison. It is part of a new milieu in criminal law where an appeal can be processed and denied all the way up to the United States Supreme Court, but yet the judgment of conviction is still not final. Jailhouse lawyers encourage their peers to file frivolous petitions of all sorts and counsel their clients that freedom is all but assured. The system must change, for there is only one thing more cruel than certain punishment and that is no certitude at all.

One of the most destructive innovations that multiply the incertitude about prison time is eligibility for parole. The underlying premise of the parole system is that punishment ought to be tailored to fit the criminal, not the crime. Because legislative standards of punishment had become too rigorous, the movement for discretion in the administration of punishment within prison gained impetus until the parole system became commonplace within both state and federal criminal-law systems. The time has now come, however, to admit that discretionary lessening of punishment by dispensing paroles has failed and that the parole system must end.

Once legislatures enact a system of determinate sentences for delineated criminal behavior, and once the length of specific sentences is scrutinized and judicially approved under a strict reading of the Eighth Amendment, a sentence should not be diluted by various and sundry bureaucrats administering their own concept of substantive justice through the parole system. As William Leonard Gordon, once an inmate at New York's Auburn Correctional Facility, incisively complained, the parole system means nothing more than life on the installment plan. Once a prisoner gets tied up in the bureaucratic administration of justice by penologists, ultimate freedom is only a fanciful and illusive ideal. Rehabilitation is supposed to be the goal with freedom the final reward. Unfortunately, neither is integrated into our present parole system. It is far better to give prisoners definite times of realistic dimensions with ultimate realization of freedom upon completion of the sentence than to provide for the continuous and unending interference in an individual's life because of past criminal behavior.

Parole cannot work as anyone who has ever read a

parole contract quickly comes to realize. It is totalitarianism at its worst, completely and undisguisedly dictating to an inmate where he can go, where he must live, how he must work, whom he can see, what he may drink, and where he must report to his parole officer. Certain crime. Definite punishment. There can be no middle ground, and attempted mitigation of punishment by the parole system only fosters more evil than good. Furthermore, certain punishment without the possibility of dilution of the sentence is the only humane form of punishment that removes the anxieties of living in a state of flux where neither punishment nor reward is assured. In a system of rational punishment for crime, there is no need for parole, and a system that needs parole is admitting that the punishment is far too severe and not justified by the crime.

There is a middle-class naiveté in parole administration, which is exemplified in *Arciniega* v. *Freeman*, 404 U.S. 4, 92 S.Ct. 22, 30 L.Ed. 2d 126 (1971). At the end of 1960, Raymond Arciniega was sentenced to ten years imprisonment for selling heroin. In September, 1967, he was released from prison on parole with a little more than three years yet to be served. On March 17, 1969, Arciniega was arrested as a parole violator because he "associated with persons having criminal records." After a parole revocation hearing, he was recommitted to prison to complete the remaining time on his original sentence. The only evidence of his association with other persons with criminal records was that he was employed in a restaurant where other ex-convicts were also employed. Despite this limited on-the-job contact with ex-convicts, the parole board, the United States District Court for the Central District of California, and the United States Court of Appeals, Ninth Circuit, all held that Raymond Arciniega had violated his parole and was properly recommitted to prison. On October 31, 1971, over two-and-one-half years after his recommitment to prison, the United States Supreme Court re-instated his parole holding that mere on-the-job contact with other employee ex-convicts was not a sufficient reason for revoking Arciniega's parole.

The unrealistic expectations of the members of the parole board in the Arciniega case are symptomatic of the treatment of prisoners by the bureaucrats who administer the parole system. Imagine, it took the United States Supreme Court to tell the parole board and other judges that *working* with ex-cons ought not to be a parole violation. There is obviously an ignorance about the realities of life that allows parole boards and other judges to permit an ex-con to be locked up in jail as a parole violator for working with other ex-cons. Perhaps it is well to illustrate the life style of the normal prisoner.

After a finding of guilt, a defendant is taken from society and placed in prison. He remains there for a period of time until a parole board, or other legal equivalent, decides that the prisoner can return to society without any visible danger to its members. In order to assure society's safety, however, the parole board sets up a series of do's and don't's apparently designed to "normalize" the prisoner's life outside of jail. Essentially, the rule provides that the parolee must forget his old way of life and make a new start without the encumbrances of the past. The parolee, however, has no money and only the prospect of a second-rate job. He has spent the last several years in jail, and has no new friends on the outside who can assist him in making the adjustment from prisoner to parolee. Inevitably, he must return to old friends, old acquaintances, old neighborhoods, and an old life style. Parole boards have not yet found the formula for magically transporting parolees to the pleasures and diversions of suburbia. As the parolee drifts back into his old life style, he inevitably violates his parole. A parole violation is not necessarily a crime, and mere association with the wrong people or frequenting prohibited places can land a parolee back in prison. Once back in prison, the parolee often loses credit for the time spent out on the streets under parole supervision. Consequently, he resumes serving his sentence from the point of his last imprisonment. Hence, the impression by prisoners that the usage of parole and its unrealistic level of expectations by parole boards often amounts in practice to a life sentence by installments.

The parole system has failed. It serves neither the prisoner for whom it was designed nor the society it was intended to protect. Instead, it consumes finite resources in an overburdened criminal-justice system, which can be better used in crime detection and prosecution. It exacerbates the inequities in sentencing and only serves to foster anxiety and anguish among prisoners. It is an unsuccessful experiment in totalitarianism that has failed to resolve recidivism. The parole system must end and be replaced by a system of rational punishment of definite statutorily prescribed lengths. Only in that way will the purpose of retribution and deterrence be served by the criminal-law system.

Fourteen:

Life in Jail—
An Alternative

I remember my first time inside a prison. It was during the summer of 1969. I was working with the Cleveland public defender's office. I was sent over to the Cuyahoga County Prison to interview an inmate.

The first overwhelming sensation that I recall was breathing the stench. The odor from unwashed human bodies was overpowering. There was no air circulation inside the building and nowhere for the stench to go. It just hung there to be breathed in by all inside, guards as well as prisoners, visitors as well as permanent residents. I almost puked.

While I was waiting in a foyer for the guards to bring the inmate for the interview, five other prisoners were brought from their cells to the area to await being escorted down to the courtroom. A huge, black policeman came up to the five, and ordered another guard to take only four of them and leave one old man behind. The guard did as he was told, and the policeman began unashamedly harassing the old black man. "You and I are going to do the thing together, old man," he began. "We're going to give you a taste of prison life. Just you and me, alone and together. The thing. You and I are going to do it. And we're going to have lots of fun."

The old man just stood pushed against the wall with tears beginning to cloud his eyes. He never answered. He just listened as the harangue continued ceaselessly. Finally, another guard took the sad old man away, presumably to a courtroom.

As I remained standing there silently, another inmate walked up to me and asked if I had change for a dollar. He wanted to call a bail bondsman, and he needed a dime to make the call. I took my change out of my pocket, and found that I only had one dime and a few pennies. I told him that I was sorry, but I did not have the change, and I began to put my hand back in my pocket. He was a young man, early twenties, small and slender. As my hand went toward my pocket, he interrupted me and said, "I'll give you the dollar for the dime." I looked into his eyes, and realized just how important freedom from fear was. He did not want to spend a night in that place, where one can trust neither guards nor fellow inmates. I gave him the dime and refused the dollar, and he went quickly on his way to call a bondsman.

When I stepped out of prison that afternoon into the polluted Cleveland air, I breathed deeply and realized how sweet the taste of freedom is. My stomach still retched from the stench that I breathed inside the walls of the jail, and I walked away from it knowing that there was nothing I could do.

Years later, I walked the prison yard of Jackson State Penitentiary at Jackson, Michigan, and realized the power of the powerless. Jackson State, I was told, is the largest penitentiary in our nation, and has one of the largest prison yards. It was a warm spring day and groups of prisoners congregated in different sectors of the yard. One prisoner came running up to me and the guard I was with and asked who I was and why I was there. Once he was given his answer, he returned to his comrades to share his information. "There's really nothing we can do," the guard explained as the inmate left, "if they decide to kill us out here or take us hostage. They are in control here just because there are so many." We continued our walk among murderers, robbers, rapists, muggers, and we went unmolested. It was the power of the many against the few, and it was difficult to know who ran whom.

Jackson State also had a research institute where pharmaceutical companies tested out new drugs on human beings before the drugs were sold to the general public. Healthy men allowed other men to stick needles in their arms or pills in their mouths that made them ill. Only volunteers are used, but the supply of candidates for experimentation was always greater than the demand. The reason for the prisoner interest was simple: money, a comfortable bed, good food, and a chance to watch color TV. Life was better sick inside the research institute than it was healthy in any other place inside Jackson State.

It is a sad commentary on the prison condition that prisoners are the only substantial class of persons who are willing to serve as medical guinea pigs for drug experimentation for the rest of mankind. The problem with our prisons is that we take abnormal people, place them in an abnormal environment, demand that they live an abnormal life style, and somehow expect them to become normal from the experience. Our prisons do not work, and the reasons for their failure are rather obvious.

Prisons cannot be abolished. It is a simple but sad fact that there are members of our society who cannot live with their fellow human beings without killing, robbing, assaulting, raping, or otherwise hurting others. There is reason to believe that the cause may be biological. There is also reason to believe that the cause may stem from the inequities in our social structure. Whatever the cause, the mass of society must be protected from those who for their own reasons refuse to respect the lives and property of others.

Given the premise that there must be prisons, there still remains an infinite variety of alternatives regarding types of incarceration. Once upon a time, dungeons were used where torture was considered a legitimate part of prison routine. To some extent our society has abandoned the premise that caused dungeons to be built.

There is today a trend toward reforming prison life. Halfway houses. Behavior-modification programs. Work-release programs. Citizen parole advisors. Prisons are re-named "correctional institutes," and prisoners are called "residents" or "guests." The buildings remain the same, and life for the typical inmate is unchanged, but euphemistic names are used to smooth over the realities of the harshness of their existence. Jailhouse lawyers are now institutionalized and called "resident legal advisors." They give the same bad advice they always gave, and serve only to build up unrealistic expectation that is doomed to failure from the start. Yet, in the name of reform we get "correctional institutes," "guests," and "resident legal advisors."

If prison reform is to be a reality, it must start with basics. Prisons must be smaller, and there must be more prisons. The primary justification for prisons is that there must be places of detention where people who committed crimes against the lives and property of others must live. Such persons must be removed from society in order that others may live civilized lives. During their incarceration, it must be obvious to them that they are not in control of their lives and the *de facto* control that the powerless have merely because of their numbers must be eliminated. This can only be done if the numbers at each penal institution are kept within reasonable degrees.

Once there are more smaller prisons, the next requirement is to attempt to normalize their life styles as much as feasible. Remember, the biggest problem with prisons today is that we are dealing with abnormal people in abnormal environments living abnormal lives with the expectation that these people will somehow be normalized at the end of their incarceration.

To attempt normalization of prison life, the entire concept of prison as we know it today must be revamped. Prisons must be transformed into prison communities where an inmate can live with his spouse and family. The prisoners must be able to work either inside or outside the prison community walls where an inmate will be responsible for his own and his family's well-being. There must be schools for the prisoners, as well as for their children, where job skills and the rudiments of education can be taught. The *de facto* internal prison administration must be given a *de jure* basis where prisoners set up and control a legal system to protect themselves against their own kind. The economics of prison life must not be artificial and the economic realities of life must be the same inside and outside of prison. Professional guidance and counseling must be available to all inmates as well as to their families in order that rehabilitation be something more than a fanciful goal.

The vision of such prison communities is, of course, not all-encompassing. It is realized that, despite professional care, some people can never be rehabilitated. The effort must be made, but where failure is encountered, it must be accepted. In the case of the repeated offender, prison communities as the means of rehabilitation can no longer be used, and humane places of detention would ultimately be needed. In such instances, we must come to realize that our resources will be better spent elsewhere, and we cannot continue indefinitely to help those who will not help themselves. This harsh reality must be accepted in the case of prisoners who continually and seriously challenge the life and property of others. If they have opted for a life of perpetual crime, our society and our law must respond firmly and humanely. If detention is the only realistic answer, then houses of detention must be built. But for the criminal entrepreneur who is not yet confirmed in a life of crime, prison communities might very well be the answer to rehabilitation. A normal environment might very well produce prisoners who are prepared to return to society. It is all too obvious that the abnormalities of present prison life are not suited for that end.

A combination of prison communities and houses of detention ought to be the reality of incarceration after conviction. Such a process cannot work in our present system where legislative definition of crime is too expansive and where punishment after conviction lies in the unbridled discretion of the trial judge. Prison reform must be seen as an incidental by-product of the larger need for restructuring the criminal-law process. A realistic redefinition of criminal conduct. A return to the sacredness of the jury and its verdict. A system of realistic and definite punishment. Such are the basic changes that are vital to penal reform. Without reforming the criminal-law process itself to effect substantive justice for the prosecution and the defense, penal reform is impossible. If criminal law were to more accurately reflect the actualities of life, penal reform would be inevitable. The one flows from the other, and prisoners will only be fairly treated when society no longer fears the criminal who can steal property and a life with impunity. When criminal law becomes committed to substantive justice both for the prosecution and the defense, then penal reform will inevitably follow.

Fifteen:

Conclusion—
A Personal Note

Our criminal-law system does not work. There is a recurrent theme among modern-day commentators that the criminal-justice system is cracking down because of its own weight. The police are overburdened. Prosecutors are far too scarce. Appellate courts have created more and more loopholes for defense lawyers to exploit. Such observations are far too simplistic. They reflect an ignorance of the nuts and bolts of our criminal-justice system.

The system can be made to work. Tightening up a nut here. Loosening a bolt there. That is all it would take to make the system work. But the revitalization of our criminal-law system must start with the basics, and, for that, one must begin at the beginning and society must decide what it *expects* from criminal law.

Revenge must no longer be accepted as a legitimate end of criminal law. Attempts to camouflage revenge as retribution must be unmasked for what they are. Retribution must be recognized as basically a subjective goal that can only be approximated if the legislators make a concerted effort at treating similar offenses equally instead of similar offenders equally.

Serious efforts must be made at rehabilitation of first and second offenders, but recidivism must be recognized as the danger to civilization that it really is. Repeated criminal offenders must be placed in prisons because that is the only place where they can live without molesting the mass of civilized society.

Once the purpose is clearly articulated, then the nuts and bolts must be treated. Our current system, which requires probable cause for arrest, is as vital today as it was in 1971, and policemen who violate its standards must be held strictly accountable for its violation. Policemen ought not be allowed to kill and maim other policemen—or their fellow citizens—and then be allowed to escape punishment because of the technicalities of criminal law. There ought to be explicit statutory offenses for policemen who make grossly illegal arrests, and they ought not be allowed to serve as servants of the very law that they violate.

Search and seizure ought to be kept within the strict constitutional bounds requiring warrants where practicable and searches incident to a lawful arrest only where exigent circumstances preclude their use. Good-faith errors ought not preclude the use of unlawfully seized evidence at trial; however, where police officers continually make errors, then they ought not continue to serve as policemen.

Legislators ought to spend more time drafting criminal statutes defining the specifics of behavior that offend the property or lives of others. They should stop moralizing through the sanction of criminal law, and remember that even Jesus Christ gave man the free will to commit immoral acts. Criminal statutes ought to be strictly tailored only to particular behavior that offends the lives and property of others. Prostitutes, junkies, gamblers, pimps, sodomists, and smut peddlers may require regulation, but regulation by prohibition has *never* worked.

The focus of criminal law ought to be reset to protecting life and property, and reject ancillary goals. By that same token, criminal law must recognize its own limitations, and where reality and experience say that criminal statutes cannot protect fetal human life, then time and effort ought not be wasted in dreaming the impossible dream. Abortion, like victimless crime, may very well be an area where regulation, not outright prohibition, is the only realistic approach.

The constitutional ideal of trial by jury ought once again be invigorated. Juries should decide guilt and innocence, not prosecutors by the process of plea bargaining. By that same token, the jury ought to be given all reliable evidence indicating guilt or innocence, and other constitutional objectives ought not to be pursued at the expense of informed jury deliberations. Juries may very well make mistakes. Innocent men may be convicted and guilty men may go free. In the history of mankind, no more noble institution has ever been designed or ever implemented for the purpose of deciding guilt or innocence. But when our criminal-law system intentionally withholds reliable evidence from the jury, the process more nearly resembles medieval trial by ordeal instead of trial by informed jury deliberation. Furthermore, the jury system ought to be reinforced by mandatory jury service so that the constitutional ideal of trial by a jury of the accused's peers might be closer to reality than the hit-and-miss process of selecting panels of jurors.

While the accused is awaiting his trial by jury, the right to bail ought to be a reality. Bail bondsmen ought to be recognized for the public service they perform as well as the indispensable role they serve for the poor, the weak, and the powerless. The fact that their motives may be mercenary ought not diminish the reality of their contribution to society.

The most pressing area of reform, and the easiest to accomplish is in the area of sentencing. It is somewhat ironic that politicians and lawyers are the least regarded professionals among our citizenry, but judges who are merely lawyer-politicians wearing robes are among the most respected of all Americans. Judges have far too much unchecked power in the scheme of criminal justice today. Our constitutional system was founded on checks-and-balances and the division of governmental power among the three departments so that power can be checked by power. This same application of limited governmental power ought to function in the process of sentencing in criminal law.

In criminal law, judges serve as demigods who determine sentences with little or no real statutory guidance and without accountability to anyone. The too-harsh and too-lenient judges undermine any semblance of equality of treatment of the laws, which our nation professes as a constitutional imperative. Individual judges are responsible for the most gross violations of our ideal of equality under the law, and there is currently no way to check evil judges except by death or retirement. Lawyers who see racist judges, crooked judges, lazy judges, incompetent judges can do nothing because those very same judges ultimately determine the livelihoods of the members of the bar. Power corrupts, and absolute power corrupts absolutely, and if anyone has absolute power in criminal law today, it is American judges. Such a system ill serves the cause of justice.

Punishment in criminal law ought to be certain, and it ought not to be cruel or inhuman. Certitude is a prerequisite for deterrence, and the reason there is no real deterrence in criminal law today is because certitude of punishment is absent. Parole ought to be abolished. Prerelease programs ought to be ended. Indeterminate sentences ought to be eliminated. Sentences ought to be fixed and certain so that the hope of beating the rap, if caught, does not spring eternally. By that same token, the levels of punishment must be realistic if it is to be just and humane.

There was a time in American folklore when brilliant men dreamed of committing the perfect crime, but they could never accomplish their goal. Now, the perfect crime is the rule and catching the felon the exception, and it is not brilliant minds that plot and execute crime, but often the most stupid and wretched among us.

Today, the American folklore praises the lone defense lawyer who fights against the system and who responds to the plight of the disadvantaged, victimized defendant. Such images are, however, only myth for the real disadvantaged are the young and old, the black, the poor, and the weak who are mostly the victims of crime. Today's common criminal does not rip off the system. Instead, he steals from his neighbors or he assaults his friends because he is bigger or stronger or rougher or tougher than his victim. He is brazen and audacious because he almost never gets caught, and if he gets caught, he usually escapes punishment. It is only after he becomes enmeshed in a total commitment to crime that the criminal-law system takes note, and then attempts to place him in jail. He ought not to be idolized, and the lawyer who comes to his defense is certainly no hero. He is merely a man doing a job that has to be done because the guilty as well as the innocent deserve a defense, and a fair and impartial trial.

Such are the nuts-and-bolts of criminal law that need attention. It is not glamorous or exciting work, and it does not take huge quantities of money. The only area in criminal law that truly needs a mass infusion of funds is penal reform and the building of more, smaller, better jails. All other reform can be accomplished by a dedication to and diligence in the realities of drafting criminal laws. It is primarily a matter for the legislators of our fifty states, but they are far too accustomed to turning the problems over to Washington, and Washington thinks the only solution to human problems is throwing piles of money at them in order to make them go away. It is time that our legislators start legislating and start by repealing the errors of the past. We need new criminal codes unlike any we have ever seen. The framework is here. The nuts-and-bolts need attention. It is time someone paid attention for criminal law needs reform if there is to be justice both for the prosecution and the defense.

Index